# FROM MIRACLE TO MIRACLE
## A STORY OF SURVIVAL

BY ALICIA FLEISSIG MAGAL

# FROM MIRACLE TO MIRACLE
## A STORY OF SURVIVAL

BY ALICIA FLEISSIG MAGAL

# NIKA KOHN FLEISSIG

Outskirts Press, Inc.
Denver, Colorado

Outskirts Press, Inc.
http://www.outskirtspress.com

ISBN: 978-1-4327-6058-8

PRINTED IN THE UNITED STATES OF AMERICA

# Dedication

To my Mamusia who brought me life and always told me I brought her back to life. Your colorful, dramatic, bold personality has always inspired me and enabled me to reach beyond myself to achieve my dreams.

You showed me how to live each day as an adventure.

You are the Matriarch of three generations, and can never know how many people's lives you have touched beyond our family!

You are a blessing.

# Acknowledgements

How to bridge the gaps in my knowledge of the historical back-drop of the Second World War and the gaps in my mother's memory of the scenes of her own story during the war? I am indebted to historical experts and close family and friends who generously offered resources to fill in and explain some of the missing information about prisoner-of-war camps, the Geneva Convention, and other historical facts:

Dr. Michael Berenbaum, Holocaust historian and professor, Director of the Sigi Ziering Center for the Study of the Holocaust and Ethics at America Jewish University, Los Angeles, CA; Aaron Breitbart, Senior Researcher, Simon Wiesenthal Center, Los Angeles, CA; Ed Gaffney, producer of film Empty Boxcars, Andrew Beck, son of the pre-war Polish Foreign Minister, and longtime family acquaintance in America.

With loving gratitude to cousins Anita Chasson in Israel, Irene Goldberg in Switzerland, and Martin and Daniel Wolf in England, for assisting with identifying names, places, and dates regarding relatives on the branches of the Bierman and Kohn family tree.

To Cynthia Richmond, the leader of the Tuesday morning Book Writing Group in the Village of Oak Creek, Arizona, a huge thank you for the inspiring and supportive encouragement throughout the writing process, and to the members of the group who listened to each other read a chapter a week of our respective books with compassion, open-heartedness, and helpful comments.

To Anne Crosman, author and journalist, I want to express my admiring appreciation for her thoughtful and professional editing of the first draft of my manuscript. She became a true and valued family friend.

To patient, smiling Dr. Anita Rosenfield, many thanks for her ability to make endnotes, bibliography, synopsis and other annotations concise and clear. Her advice and encouragement helped me continue when I encountered technical challenges.

To Larry Gray, Colleen, and the team of Outskirts Press, much gratitude for their expert and enthusiastic advice throughout the whole publishing process.

To the congregants of the Jewish Community of Sedona and the Verde Valley in Sedona, Arizona, where I serve as rabbi and spiritual leader, my thanks for embracing me and my family. You have offered much encouragement to finish the book, and provided me with opportunities to read parts of it for Holocaust memorial ceremonies. All my learning and life experiences are finding expression in this extraordinary community.

To my husband, Itzhak, brother Will, and children Tali and Amir, who asked important questions that led me to probe deeper and expand some of the chapters with additional factual and emotional details, I express my deep thanks. Their encouragement and loving support kept me on track when I got distracted. Amir designed the cover and offered his assistance with the photos, documents, and maps. I am most grateful to him for his artistic and technical contributions.

And to my mother Nika, who is truly an inspiration to us, her close family, and to all whom she meets, thank you for surviving, giving me life, and encouraging me to tell this story of survival, hope, and healing. I have dedicated my life to bringing joy through Judaism to the next generation, in great part, because of my wish to bring forth a new vibrant branch from the nearly-severed trunk of our individual family tree as well as the communal Jewish tree cut down so brutally. Because of my mother I cherish the stories of the past as I look to the future.

# Review of Book

by Dr. Michael Berenbaum, Holocaust historian and
professor, Director of the Sigi Ziering Center for
the Study of the Holocaust and Ethics at America
Jewish University, Los Angeles, California:

*From Miracle to Miracle: A Story of Survival* is a book of intensity
and intimacy. Rabbi Alicia Fleissig Magal narrates the story of
her mother's survival in the Holocaust through a series of vi-
gnettes in which the daughter's experiences trigger her mother's
revelations. The full story only emerges over time, and only in
fragments, indeed the way in which one remembers. We learn of
mother and daughter, of two worlds so distinct in time and circumstances that they are universes apart but linked by the love of
a mother for daughter and a daughter for her mother."

# Table of Contents

The introductory paragraph of each chapter portrays an incident in my life which led to my mother's opening up about an episode in her story of survival. My mother Nika's narrative appears in an *italic font* to create a difference between my voice and hers.

Introduction ................................................................................. i

The Red Line: Perspective of Second Generation,
   Children of Holocaust Survivors ............................................ iii

The Bicycle:
*1935 Fall From Bicycle Leads to Vienna* ................................. 1

I Recognize You:
*1939 She Recognized Me and That Put Me in Danger* .......................... 5

The Painting:
*1939 He Loved the Portrait and Took My Room* ................................. 7

Prom Dress:
*1939 From Queen of the Ball to Cockroach* ................................. 9

Fascinated with the Paranormal:
*1939 Psychic Foretelling: You Will Be All Right* .................................. 13

Seeking Names for the Family Tree:
*1940-42 Our Family, Trying to Stay Together*................................... 17

Zosia Pozniak:
*1942 My Piano Teacher Saved My Life*.................................... 23

Telephone Numbers and Addresses:
*1943 Remember My Address* ...................................... 29

People-Watching:
*1943 The Smell of Fear* ........................................ 31

A Kosher Meal:
*1943 A Kosher Meal? Identity Discovered* ............................... 35

Underground in Paris:
*1944 Maze of Tunnels Underneath the City of Warsaw*.................... 39

Birthday Party:
*1944 One Memorable Birthday*........................................ 41

Nothing to Eat:
*1944 Starved Out*................................................ 43

Soup:
*1944 Soup, Food, Barter*............................................ 47

Drug Education:
*1944 Prisoner of War Camp*......................................... 51

Love Letters in the Attic:
*1944-1945 Love Letters*............................................ 53

President Roosevelt:
*1945 Liberation*................................................. 55

In American Uniform:
*1945 Useful in Uniform* ....................................................... 59

Fashion Drawing:
*1945 Documents, Drawing, and Delays* ............................... 65

Sixth Sense; She Just Knew:
*1945 I Knew It Was Time To Go* .......................................... 71

Greetings After an Absence:
*1946 First Commercial: Chiquita Banana* ........................... 75

How Did You Meet Your Husband?:
*1946 I Met My Husband in New York* .................................. 79

Intimate Stranger .................................................................... 85

Reaching Back ........................................................................ 87

Postscript ................................................................................ 91


Appendix- Warsaw Uprising, Prisoners of War,
Geneva Convention, maps of Poland, etc. ........................... 97

End notes, Historical Information ......................................... 101

Bibliography of Suggested Books on Children of the Holocaust
and Children of Holocaust Survivors ................................... 111

Photos .................................................................................... 114

# Introduction

The whole family was gathered for a family vacation at my mother's cottage in Wellfleet, Cape Cod. My mother picked up the printed copy of the first draft of the book about her story of survival during World War Two which I had brought for her to read when we could work on it, and clear up mistakes and clarify some details. After she finished reading it, she emerged from her bedroom teary-eyed. She said, "I read this book as if it is an adventure about someone else. And I wonder, 'How will it turn out?' "

I laughed and pointed to the full room of people, most of whom owe their existence to her: my brother William with his wife Wendy and children, Ariel and Mia; Will's son David, our daughter Tali and her soon-to-be-husband Craig, and our son Amir, and I wave my hand at the laughing crowd of contented, loving people from age four to over sixty. "Mom, THIS is how it turned out!" She responded wistfully, with a combination of tears and smiles, "I lived through these wartime experiences and I can't believe half of it really happened! It is like a dream. It is truly such a miracle that I survived. I'm so glad I lived to see our family grow again, and be loving and close to each other."

# The Red Line

My mother's name at birth was Bronislawa Felicia Kohn. By the time I was born, her name had become Nika Fleissig. The transformation between the two names included losing her entire family, escaping death many times, living with assumed names on false papers, moving to a new country after World War Two, and getting married.

I learned about my mother's incredible stories in short fragments during ordinary events in my life, which brought up memories for her. Like many Second Generation Children of Holocaust Survivors, I was deeply impacted by her experiences. Her messages molded my character and influenced my decisions.

As a young girl and teenager, if I got upset over a pimple, or a B+ rather than an A on a test, or had problems with a boyfriend once I started to date, I felt guilty. How did I dare allow myself to get sad or angry over such small challenges, compared to what my mother had gone through? It was hard to take my own "small life" seriously, in comparison with the life and death perspective of my beautiful and brave mother.

Each time some seemingly small incident occurred in my life -- when I learned to ride a bike, put pictures in an album, listened to a TV commercial -- really random moments, my mother got "that look," and I knew there was an opening back to That Time Before. Some of the "trigger conversations" happened only once. Others were repeated many times, and each time with a different slant, and more details that filled out the story in a new way. I stayed very still, as I knew I was about to get a glimpse into that earlier world that existed in her life before the Red Line.

Red Line? That is the vivid image I held in my child's mind of a large page that illustrated my family history. At the top are names of many, many relatives, representing the normal, happy life of my mother's extended family before World War Two. And then there is a thick horizontal Red Line across the page. Underneath that line there is a new picture: The Mother, The Father, The Daughter, The Son. And scattered at the edges of the page are a few small figures of various far-off great aunts, second cousins, and friends with Polish names, who stood in for relatives. I lived in that tight cluster below the Red Line.

In 2007, at the age of 87, my mother had her first art exhibit of paintings, a retrospective of her oil and watercolor portraits and landscapes that she had painted over the past 50 years. I wrote a short bio about her for the newspapers. Several people who read the article said, "You should write a book about her, and tell her fascinating story." I agreed, but how could I write her story? She never expressed any emotions when retelling her near misses with death during the war. She offered only brief segments of events at odd moments when something prompted a memory.

I have read many Holocaust survivors' books, and marveled that the survivors could set down the words with such candor, such clear memory, including their feelings, and the order of events.

One source to which I could turn for some rough chronology was a three-hour video of my mother's testimony in a very caring interview by Rosalie Franks for Steven Spielberg's Shoa Foundation. However, I was hesitant to ask my mother to explore those memories with me. I knew that experience of reliving the war years through the Shoa interview had drained her for days. The same year she spoke to fifth graders who were studying the Holocaust in a school on Nantucket Island near her Cape Cod summer home. Judging from the moving thank-you letters the students sent her, she had offered a very inspiring talk, but the toll on her was high. She could not sleep for several nights afterward, and decided not to do any more speaking. It took too much out of her. I hesitated to propose working on a book project about her world before and during World War Two. Wouldn't it plunge her into that nightmare again?

When I was a teenager, my father had told me that he never asked certain questions of my mother, even though she was his wife. Could I intrude now, asking about those dark years? The bits and pieces I had gleaned, even the additional information in the video, are not the whole story. She is now 89 years old. Virtually all her contemporary relatives and friends are gone. And she is asking me, "Alisienko, Please write this book." Now she is more motivated to document what she went through.

Each story I heard over the years added another tiny chapter. Like so many frayed strings and threads knotted together, they form a thicker cord. I wanted to hold on to that lifeline and feel connected to her and the unknown namesakes that gave my brother and me our names: Alicia for her mother Amalia, and Berthold, her brother, for my brother William's middle name.

Although I grew up in the 1960's, life was not about sex, drugs, and rock 'n roll. Far from embracing a hippy lifestyle, I was careful, did not take risks, never rebelled, did not participate in demonstrations or protests, and avoided bringing further sadness or worry to my parents. "They had suffered and lost enough." That was my unspoken rule and internal understanding, even though my parents never spoke those words to me.

When I lived in Jerusalem in my 20's, I read the book *Second Generation: Children of Holocaust Survivors* by Helen Epstein. For the first time I felt that I was part of a group that had a name. I felt a connection with people who shared a similar background. That reading of *Second Generation* was a turning point in my life. It rained for two days and I immersed myself in the book, as my tears matched the outside weather.

While I read, I imagined hundreds, maybe thousands of other young people growing up, listening to wartime stories of their parents and reacting in a many ways to specific tales of loss and horror. They understood! Their parents all had accents. Their mothers cooked food with unusual tastes and smells, different from tuna-noodle casseroles, hamburgers, and peanut butter-and-jelly sandwiches at friends' homes. Our survivor parents had suffered. They stood for an heroic ideal above that which we saw in "regular" American homes with more lenient rules and less complicated dynamics.

It is not surprising that a huge percentage of Second Generation Children of Holocaust Survivors (I feel I must capitalize this description) entered the helping professions as therapists, social workers, specialized teachers, rabbis, cantors, and others who try to assist others compassionately. Perhaps it was an effort to "rescue" them. It is possible that many of us felt a strong need to heal, to repair what was broken, to uplift those in pain, since we could not go back in time and pluck our own parents out of danger.

Even in my 30's, 40's, and 50's, I felt I was living in the shadow of my mother's accomplishments. People have called me a pioneer. They admired my going back to school in my 40's and becoming a rabbi. My reaction was often, "Who me? Brave? A pioneer? You are interested in my story?!" For me, the story was always *my mother's story*, especially in her late teens and early 20's.

I had always been a good girl who listened to the rules and abided by them. Although that won me praise at home and in school, I knew that the very same trait considered very positive and commendable would have led to my death during the war. I most likely would have marched quietly with all the others in a long line bound for the gas chamber. My mother thought for herself, went her own way, and decided for herself which direction to take. That independent thinking and strong belief in her own instinct contributed to her survival.

Several childhood scenes vividly come to mind and demonstrate her ability to buck the crowd, the current mode of accepted thinking, and do things her own way, with a sense of humor.

■ I'm ten years old, and rehearsing for a play in religious school at the Jewish Community Center in White Plains, N.Y. The script calls for my character to appear in "street clothes." My mother is sewing my costume, a bright red full skirt and bodice, with shiny ribbon trim. I hold up the script, and say doubtfully, "Mommy, it says here 'street clothes.' Isn't this dress too fancy?" "Well, she replies, they didn't say *which* street. This dress is for Fifth Avenue!" And that's how I appeared in the play.

■ At the ragged, soggy edges of winter's end, my mother starts a tradition in our family. It celebrates the anniversary of her arriving in the USA on the 14th of February, 1946, and my father's birthday on the 15th. It is a time of year when my brother Willy and I are pale and lacking energy. My mother decides the whole family should go skiing. But what about school? Not a problem. She makes an appointment with the principal, tells him of her plan to remove us from school for ten days, and assures him that we will take our homework with us, and return with enthusiasm to our studies. He doesn't like the idea, but finally he acquiesces. My mother dismisses the school authorities and the entire educational system in America as "creating mediocrities." I am struck by her individualistic way of thinking. While the principal doesn't openly express his disapproval, I notice that I do not receive a star for attendance those years, even though I don't miss other days.

We drive to North Conway, New Hampshire, each year from the time I am ten until age 14. I take ski class in the morning, advancing each couple of days to a higher class, and then skiing down the slopes with my brother and parents each afternoon. We look like a curving row of ducks arranged by height - first Daddy, then Mommy, then I, and finally my little brother Willy. My mother cares greatly about anything that promotes our stamina. "This exercise will keep you healthy for the whole year, and give you a skill in a sport. You just never know what knowledge will come in handy in your life." Later I find out that her athletic ability and strength helped her survive during harsh wartime conditions.

▪ Willy and I are enrolled in Red Cross swimming classes at Gull Pond in Wellfleet, Cape Cod where we spend most summers. We learn to swim methodically, and advance to new levels after mastering new strokes and swimming more laps. My mother, by contrast, had taught herself to swim, without any classes or coaching. As a very young girl, she observed champion swimmers in the Park Krakowski near her home in Krakow, Poland. She had a very strong sense, "If they can do it, so can I."

She put a cork belt around her chest and threw herself into the water, imitating the strokes she saw. Over and over she tried, and slowly developed a smooth swimming stroke. Her style became so perfect that a professional trainer asked if she wanted to train for competitions. Although she was only eight years old, she already was definite in her refusal to train competitively. She loved the sport for its own sake, and didn't care for groups. She swam for pleasure, not competition. This trait of learning on her own, without need for outside assistance or encouragement, served her well during the war.

I gained more insights about my mother as I grew up. Each new piece of her story helped me know her better. Each was a window into the years before and during the war. It is through these "trigger scenes" in my life that I will write about my mother's life. I will write her words as she spoke them, and try to capture her accent and unique voice. I will tell how an anecdote I thought I already knew was presented again from a different point of view, with an additional moral to the story. I will write my story in regular typeface as a short introduction to each chapter, and my mother's narrative will follow in italics.

My mother, Nika Fleissig, is a very colorful character. Her face retains its beauty and expressiveness. She still has a great figure, with long legs, and a confident walk. She is always beautifully dressed, favoring slacks and attention-grabbing blouses, shawls, and jewelry from her travels around the world. She speaks easily with anyone she meets about her opinions on not wasting food or money, eating only the freshest, tastiest foods, the delights of travel (off-season, of course), and the importance of art and expression in one's life. People who meet her are fascinated by her life, her art, her adventures, and her dramatic style. It is beyond the scope of this book to describe her life after the war and up to today. I will focus on her life from age 15 in 1935 to her 30's in the 1950's. It is a story of her survival, from one miracle to another.

# 1

# The Bicycle

I'm about 6 and a half years old. I'm thrilled to have received my first two-wheeler, a blue-green 20 inch Schwinn bicycle, with bell, reflectors, and kick stand. We are across the street from our house, in the large parking lot of the Jewish Community Center on Soundview Avenue in White Plains, New York (now Kol Ami congregation), a perfect place to practice riding my bicycle. My father, Alfred Fleissig, usually so formally dressed in suit and hat, is spending time on a Sunday helping me learn to balance for the first time without the training wheels, by holding the back of the bike, running a few steps, and then letting go as I wobble and regain balance. He claps as I succeed for longer stretches at a time. I come home flushed, tired, and triumphant. Mommy was watching us through the window and saw me as I began to ride with increasing confidence.

## 1935 - Fall from a Bicycle Leads to Vienna

*You are so lucky to learn now, when you can fall and get up, and not be afraid of trying. My mother Amalia (everyone called her Mala) protected me and constantly worried that I would hurt myself. The result was so much worse than she could have expected! When I was 15, I had still not learned to ride a bike. A very tall boy from a three-week summer camp lent me his. He held the seat as I got on and tried to pedal. Suddenly, he let go, and I couldn't keep my balance. The seat was far too high for me, so I couldn't touch the ground to stop myself with my foot. I fell hard on the gravel and broke my hip. The leg was moving and shifting. The local Polish doctor told my parents that I would have to wear a black boot because my legs were now uneven, and I would have a severe limp. My father refused to accept that. He carried me in his arms and took me by train to Vienna to see a surgeon who held out some hope. Since it was nearly impossible to get passports in Poland, we used his brother's and niece's passports. My whole dowry was spent on this trip, because of the many expenses of travel and care, even though the doctor didn't charge for the actual surgery, which was still highly experimental at that time.*

*How could I have known that in the next compartment on that train to Vienna was a woman who would later be a secretary in Oberlangen, the prisoner-of-war camp where I would be held, living under an assumed name, during the final half year of the war? But she never betrayed my true identity. We met at our friend Dziunia (June) Ellington's home on Long Island many years later and the whole story came out. There were many such strange accidental crossings of paths that occurred during the war.*

*I spent months in the hospital in Vienna, on my back in traction after the experimental operation by the now legendary Dr. Boehler, a well-known pioneer in the field of orthopedic surgery. The pain and discomfort were intense, but it was the only way to avoid having one leg much shorter than the other and being a cripple for life. I then graduated to a full cast from my hip to my toes and hobbled around for several months, during which time I lived in*

# THE BICYCLE

a palatial home of my father's sister Mala Wolf nee Kohn and my cousin Mundi (Edmund) Wolf, whom I came to idolize and adore. He was already a "mature man" in his twenties, a writer, and surrounded by actors and bohemian types who smoked and appeared extremely exotic to a protected, innocent teenager. What I loved was that he allowed me to enter his magic circle and treated me like a person, not an annoying, invisible pest. After the war, he became a very well-known writer and playwright for the BBC.

In Vienna I increased my knowledge of written and spoken German. I couldn't have known how vital that fluency would become. I observed an increasing number of "brown shirts," Nazi groups, marching in the streets. This experience offered me a wider perspective of the serious danger looming ahead, much more than my parents had in Poland. But I was just a teenager. What could I know? Once I returned to my home in Krakow, I tried to act to save our family and try to convince them to flee from Poland to a neutral country, but my fears were pushed aside by seemingly older, wiser people. At that time they could not imagine the unthinkable danger about to descend.

But for the time being, my focus was on giving my leg time to heal. Since I was still growing, the constricting cast caused my left foot to be a size smaller than the right, and the left leg about an inch shorter than the right one. From the time of the operation in 1935 until the war broke out, I had shoes made to order, twice a year by Warner, a fine shoemaker who made each pair to order: a new pair at Rosh Hashanah and another at Passover. Rather than a horrible limp, I merely had a slight wiggle when I walked. After the war when I lived in America where one bought ready-made shoes in fixed sizes, I had to buy shoes in the size of the larger foot and get every pair of shoes fitted with a lift to make the left foot fit into the larger shoe. Sometimes a pair of shoes was inexpensive enough that I could buy two pairs of the same style in two different sizes, and just use the ones that fit each foot!

# FROM MIRACLE TO MIRACLE

*I know that if I had not had the operation, I never would have survived the war. It is an absolute miracle that I had this newly-developed operation, and healed well enough to survive the war, get married, and have children. All because of those two seconds on the too-tall bike. That is why I want you to learn sports and try new things. I must not over-protect you. That is the REAL protection, teaching you how to do things on your own!*

Postscript: When my mother was 85, she had her right hip replaced. She asked the surgeon to lengthen the shorter leg and make it even with the other one. For the first time in 70 years her legs were the same length. She was so excited! She had all the lifts taken out of her shoes!

# 2

# I Recognize You!

I'm 16, rehearing for a ballet recital along with students from other high schools. "Mom, guess what? I met a girl who remembers me from camp when I was eleven. Isn't that weird! I never knew she lived in the next town." My mother got that far-away smile and replied, "Sometimes being recognized can be a life-saver, and other times, it can nearly cost you your life." I could feel a story coming.

## 1939 - She Recognized Me, and That Put Me in Danger

*My father Beno's handshake meant more than a written contract. Well-respected, Benjamin Kohn had a name worth more than gold. But every family has its black sheep, and my father had a younger brother Monek, who had the opposite reputation: one day a millionaire and the next a pauper. Monek attracted women with his good looks, and had all kinds of shady business dealings. My father had nothing at all to do with him. Once, Monek got into financial difficulty and had to leave Vienna for Krakow, since he had been born in Poland, and had no citizenship papers to remain in Vienna. He needed money, and asked my father to cosign for a loan. Knowing full well that the loan would never be repaid, my father refused. That deepened the rift between them. One day out of the blue while we still lived in Krakow, Monek contacted my mother and asked her to let me to come to his home in Krakow for a holiday dinner, perhaps around Christmas. He kept insisting, and finally my parents relented and allowed me to go. Why, I really do not know. It was strange. He was not wearing an armband with a Jewish star, as we all had to do. He had an elegant Viennese girlfriend who knew where he had hidden a lot of merchandise from some business dealings. His guests were a German couple with whom he had these dealings. I don't remember much about the visit, and returned home to my parents and brother. This seemingly random event had enormous consequences later on.*

*At about this time, all young men were called to go to forced labor. My brother Toldek, the nickname of his full name Josef Berthold, was then about 18 years old, and had to respond. My parents found a Ukrainian doctor who was willing to provide my brother with a certificate saying that he had some medical condition and should not be called to forced labor. By chance, Uncle Monek's girlfriend, whom I had met at the party, happened to meet that Ukrainian doctor. She may have asked for advice on relieving someone of forced labor duty. Somehow those two conspired to keep Monek in jail. He had been put there and was to be released the very next day. Who knows? Maybe they had a plan to get rid of Monek and split up his hidden wealth. I have no idea who said what to which authorities, but one day, detectives came to our house in Bie-zanow, and claimed that I had had an affair with this Ukrainian doctor. They threatened to arrest me. I looked at them in astonishment — it was all so surreal --and spoke up in a way I had never done before in my young and innocent life. "This is not true! If you want to take me to the hospital for an examination, then do it. I have had no relationship with that man….I am a virgin." My shocked manner must have convinced them, because they left me alone and went away. That time, I was able to avoid disaster.*

# 3

# The Painting

My mother painted a beautiful oil painting of a ballerina with a long costume, a ribbon around her neck, pink ballet slippers, and brunette curls. I loved to gaze at that painting. One day, I said, "I really love that painting. I'm glad you hung it in my room." She answered, "You never know what importance a painting in your room may have." She looked far away and told me about another portrait.

### 1939 - He Loved the Portrait and Took My Room

*Rosner, the best photographer in Krakow, had made a life size portrait of me in a beautiful dress that I had worn to a ball when I was 18. I had it hanging in my bedroom in our apartment in Krakow.*

*In 1939, when the Germans entered Krakow, officials and officers took over rooms in Jewish people's houses. Later, if they needed more space, they demanded the entire building. At the beginning of the war, Mr. Kuban, a German lawyer who was general prosecutor for the whole province of Gali-*

cia, was posted at our home. He knew nothing about Jews and was not an ideological Nazi. He liked and respected my father, and they spoke together about history, philosophy, and other subjects. When he first had entered my room, he said, "What a breathtaking portrait. I'd like this room." Even though we had taken out all the good furniture from there, he still wanted that room, because of the portrait of me.

I had to sleep elsewhere, so my family arranged that I could go every night to the home of my piano teacher, Zofia (Zosia) Pozniak. We knew Zosia was a devout Catholic, a caring person, who would prove to be loyal and helpful to me again during the war, even when her husband, a professor of musicology at the University of Krakow, was imprisoned with other professors shivering outside in the cold January weather, and she was left alone with her two young children. Zosia had a very kind heart. Her mother had taught French to the young man who would become Pope John Paul II years later, but in those days was still known as Karol Wojtila. Early in the war, he was shot, and her family had nursed him back to health since he couldn't be moved far, and Zosia's family lived close to where he was treated. This was when he still had aspirations to be an actor, before dedicating his life to the Church. Consistently kind and generous, Zosia agreed to let me spend each night at her apartment. Soon, another German official took over another room in the apartment, and some time after that, our family had to leave the apartment completely. Mr. Stanislaw (Stasiu) Duda, my father's long-time socialist friend, a leader of the Polish Peasant party, came to load up some of our furniture and belongings in his horse-drawn cart, and helped us move out of Krakow to the countryside. But that's a whole other chapter. I wonder what ever happened to that beautiful portrait.

# 4

# Prom Dress

My mother and I worked on finishing and hemming a long dress from a pattern I had picked out for my high school prom. She said, "One moment a young girl goes to a dance, and who can predict what her life will be like a few months afterward? Everything you have can be taken away, and only what is in your head is really yours; only what you know, and can make with your own hands, belongs to you."

## 1939 - From Queen of the Ball to Cockroach

*My cousin, Anita Johannes, came to visit from Rzeszow, two hours to the east by train. It was the Fall of 1939. I was 19 and she was maybe 18. Anita was very frightened of all the rules and edicts. The newest was that we had to wear a yellow Star of David on our clothing. At the end of our street was a theater, where an opera was being presented, but for Germans only. Even Poles were not permitted, and certainly no Jews!!! Just a few months earlier, dressed in a frothy white gown, I had been named Queen of the Ball at a medical students' formal dance held in a fancy hall. How could it be that just a few months later, after the Germans marched in and took over Krakow without a shot being fired, I was considered less than human, a cockroach, vermin?!*

*I sat down and put to use the sewing skills I had just gained in those months after graduation, when we were unable to study or make any plans, as it was clear that war was imminent. I sewed two capes, one for Anita and one for myself. I declared, "We are going to the opera. I want to hear 'Aida.'" We threw the capes over our clothes to cover the yellow star that marked us as Jews. She was shaking with fear, but I wanted to prove that we were normal human beings, and had the right to attend a cultural event. I jeopardized the lives of both us and our families. I walked in with Anita like I owned the world. The Germans did look at us, but only as one looks at pretty girls. I thought, "How stupid they are. They think they can tell who we are." I must say I thoroughly enjoyed the opera, the first I ever attended in my life. Anita was petrified throughout the whole thing. "Let's go, let's go now," she kept pestering me.*

*When we returned home, my parents were horrified. How could I have put both of us in such danger?! Nobody believed that anyone would jump into the lion's den on purpose. But I did. I just could not accept these dehumanizing laws that reduced us, from students, workers, friends, citizens, and good neighbors to subhuman rats. If only we had known that this dehumanizing process would continue. But what was to follow was truly unimaginable, truly inconceivable at that time! Oh, if only I had convinced my loving mother and my clever father to find a route of escape then, right at the beginning! But as each new edict was proclaimed, it brought us down another notch, and finally it stripped us of any means of running away to a new life together in safety.*

*Perhaps I was able to survive because I was such a rebel and didn't follow the*

# PROM DRESS

*rules. From a pampered young girl I slowly emerged into a strong, indepen-*
*dent woman, since very soon I would be left with no parents or brother, no*
*money, no home, no possessions or protection, only a knowledge of languages*
*and a sixth sense of whom to trust. I was also blessed with incredible luck,*
*help from friends and strangers at critical moments of mortal danger, and an*
*inexplicable certainty that I would survive.*

*As I look back, I see that I survived from miracle to miracle.*

# 5

# Fascinated with the Paranormal

I'm a teenager, fascinated by stories of mystical experiences. After spending a weekend with a very creative and colorful mother of a close friend, I approach my mother. "Mom, did you know that Eve's mother is psychic? She is studying paranormal phenomena. It is so interesting. Do you believe that people can know things that aren't logical, even before they happen?" She looks away, somewhere over my head, picks up my hand, and holds it.

## *1939 - Psychic Foretelling: You Will Be All Right*

*At the beginning of the war, my father, Benjamin Kohn, who was a philosopher, a very logical, straight-thinking, serious man, came home and said, "I want you to see a woman who is a psychic and graphologist." This was out of character for him, but I never thought of questioning his request.*

*I had just received a letter from Janek, my boyfriend since childhood. He had escaped, joined the French army, and was now in a prisoner of war camp. I had placed his latest letter in my pocket before reading it or shar-*

*ing the news with my parents. Janek was the son of a lawyer. We were unofficially engaged; we had an understanding that we would one day marry. His maternal uncle, Artur Rodzinski, was a famous conductor and music director of the New York Philharmonic Orchestra in New York. Just as the war was breaking out, in September, 1939, Janek had jumped over to our house and said, "I am running away over the border toward Romania. Whoever survives and needs help should contact my uncle Rodzinski in New York." Janek joined the French army, was captured, and became a prisoner of war in Germany near Berlin. We sent him packages when we could. Years later I found out that he tried to escape several times, and was put into solitary confinement. He had a picture of me, and an artist in the camp made a painting from that photo. But that was still in the future.*

*My father said to go to this psychic, and gave me the name and address. The woman told me to empty my head of every thought. She held my hand and proceeded to relate to me everything, about the letter and its contents, about Janek, about our family, about me, things no one could have known. Later, in 1942, shortly before were rounded up and transported, she suddenly appeared at our apartment in the village of Wieliczka, where we had been staying since 1940, in hopes that the danger would pass and we could return to our home. This psychic woman, who had met me at the very start of the war, held the hands of my mother Mala, my father Beno, and my brother Toldek. I asked her, "Why don't you also hold my hand?" She looked at me, and in a soft but clear voice replied, "You will be all right." Mr. Kuban, the general prosecutor of Galicia who had taken over our apartment in Krakow, came to say goodbye. At the time, we didn't realize that it was a goodbye. Perhaps he had advance knowledge of the transport that was about to take place.*

## FASCINATED WITH THE PARANORMAL

*I held onto that moment and those words -- that I would be all right throughout the war -- when it looked like there was simply no way out of danger, that death could come at any moment. I survived from miracle to miracle, as if I were a character in some dream story, so unreal did it all seem.*

# 6

## Seeking Names for the Family Tree

Never having met my own grandparents, I always craved them. My brother and I carried their names, but had never known the joy of knowing our parents' parents. I was named Alicia Susan for my mother's mother Amalia (Mala) and my father's mother Selma. My brother, William Berthold, was named for my father's father Wolf and my mother's brother Berthold (Toldek). Sometimes we asked about our namesakes, so that we'd have some image, some qualities, some stories to make those relatives seem real to us. In sixth grade, I was working on a family tree and asked about my mother's father. Somehow, I had heard more stories about my mother's mother, one of eight sisters and four brothers, but very little about Nika's father. My mother sat down next to me at the dining room table. She looked at the large sheet of paper where I had drawn a bare-branched tree, waiting to be adorned with scraps of paper with Polish names written on them. Later I pasted them down, but at this moment I positioned Amalia Bierman Kohn next to Benjamin Kohn, above the name of my mother, Bronislawa Felicia Kohn, and listened, as my mother gazed at the names of so many cut off so young, and said...

# FROM MIRACLE TO MIRACLE

## *1940-42 - Our Family, Trying to Stay Together*

*My father Beno was a very kind man. He loved sports. He was a Socialist who truly believed in equality for all people, and had many friends of all kinds, from peasants to aristocrats. One good friend for many years was Stanislaw Duda, head of the Polish Peasant Party. They had discussed politics and been to each other's homes. When the war broke out, Mr. Duda arrived with a cart and horse at our apartment in Krakow, helped us load some furniture and clothes, and transported us to his own home in Bierzanow in the countryside, about half way between Krakow and the salt mine area of Wieliczka. I realized then that sometimes one gets help not because of anything one has done, but because of love and respect someone has for your parents. Whatever good I may do, will hopefully be returned to my children.*

*After a short time, we could no longer stay with the Duda family in Bierzanow. The Germans issued an edict that all Jews had to move to a designated area in Wieliczka, a nearby village famous for its salt mines. These people were Jewish owners of Krakow businesses. Their stores and factories in the city had been taken over by Germans. The true word was "stolen" by the Germans. There were also refugees from Vienna and Berlin, all attempting to "wait out" the madness of the war, and hoping it would soon pass and they could return to their regular lives.*

*The Jewish owners of the businesses like my father, who had a hardware store, were of no use to the German occupiers, who instantly became the bosses and reaped all the profits. Unlike the Jewish owners, Jewish workers were still needed to keep those businesses going, but they were not allowed to live in the city itself. They were moved into the ghetto in one section of Krakow, and came into the city center to work every day.*

# SEEKING NAMES FOR THE FAMILY TREE

*Our family waited with so many others in Wielicka, not knowing whether we were safe or still in danger. Our loyal family friend Mr. Duda thought there was a chance of obtaining false documents for our family to enable us to move to a safer place. So, without any Star of David on my clothing, I traveled with Mr. Duda to Zakopane, a ski resort where I had spent many happy family vacations in years past. Now I was there on urgent business: to acquire forged papers for our family so we could escape from Poland across some border to safety. When I returned, wearing a beautifully embroidered white fur jacket that I had bought at the resort, and gave these precious documents to my father, he stood up tall and proclaimed: "I am a good citizen. I was a decorated officer of the Austrian army.[1] Nothing can happen to us. I want to die at home in my own bed." And he tore up the documents and stayed where he was. How could he have ever known how far from the truth that prediction would be? Most people thought as my father did, that after a few months of suffering we would survive and the Germans would be beaten. He couldn't imagine the unthinkable horrors that were to come. My brother Toldek and I never considered leaving our parents, although we might have been able to escape to Hungary as many did.*

*We adapted. My mother bought gold chains with the money we still had from my father's business, a store for hardware and housewares in Krakow. She was able to trade this gold to the peasants for chicken, for butter, for necessities. My mother fed many people in Wieliczka besides our family. Some were actors. Often after dinner they put on readings and plays. This was the first time I heard the magical stories of the author Shalom Aleichem in the pure and dramatic Lithuanian-accented Yiddish. I was fascinated by the sound of the Yiddish language, which we had not spoken at home. Since Yiddish combines many words from medieval German and ancient Hebrew, I was able to understand most of what was said, since I had studied Hebrew in school, and had learned German grammar at school and had perfected my spoken*

# FROM MIRACLE TO MIRACLE

*German during that year in Vienna when I was 15. These talented actors kept practicing their craft for a time when they could again appear on stage after the war. For virtually all of them, that day would never come.*

*My brother Toldek cut his hair very short so there were no curls. He believed this would make him look less Jewish, according to the stereotyping of the Nazis. No one wanted to stand out or be noticed and cause attention that could lead to being arrested on any pretext during this time when edicts were devoid of sense or morality. I took some training as a practical nurse, so I could do something helpful during wartime. We all did what we could while we waited.*

*The Germans told the Jewish authorities who helped organize and coordinate the Jewish population in Wielicka to create a hospital within two days and put all the old people there. What sounded like a humanitarian gesture turned out to be a practical solution for the Germans, who simply wanted to eliminate the elderly and infirm. Then, in the very early morning hours, Germans took them all from their beds, loaded the aged and ill Jews from that newly-created "hospital" onto carts, threw them into a ditch, and covered them, alive. They rounded everyone else up in an "aktion," and forced thousands of people to the central square of Wielicka in front of the town hall.*

*There was an ocean of people. We were told we would be transported to work somewhere to the east. Trucks were waiting to be loaded with all these people. I was standing in a very long line with my mother, father, and brother. A Polish policeman took me by the hand, pulled me out of the line, and sat me down in the passenger seat next to the lorry [truck] driver. That is the last time I ever saw my parents. I didn't get a chance to say goodbye. That moment haunts me to this day. I never got to hold their hands, embrace them, or hear their voices one last time. Late that night everyone in the long line of trucks was dropped off at a train station, and herded onto waiting trains.[2]*

# SEEKING NAMES FOR THE FAMILY TREE

*I saw nothing of this, but heard that it got very quiet. It was around midnight. I remained seated up front, next to the driver. If anyone stopped him, he said I was his girlfriend, and they let us continue on the road. I was completely silent, in shock. I sat there in a daze with no purse, no money, no handkerchief, nothing. It was early autumn, and I didn't even have a coat.*

*The driver arrived at the edge of the Blonie, a huge park on the outskirts of Krakow where I had gone horseback riding and enjoyed picnics and swimming with my family countless times before the war. It was about 5 a.m., before the nighttime curfew was lifted. Nothing would be stirring before 7 a.m., since it was a death sentence to be found walking around at such an hour. The driver opened the door, pointed toward the park, and said, "You may go." Go? Numb, I began to walk, expecting to be shot at any second. I continued walking through the park to the edge of the city limits of Krakow to my piano teacher's home, the only safe place I could think of that was close by. Zosia Pozniak had helped me in the past. I trusted her. My mother Mala had left some money and warm fur coats with her as a safe repository. We had agreed that she would be the meeting point of information and resources in case any of the family could return to Krakow. Her husband was a well-known university professor of musicology, currently in prison as a political prisoner, since all professors and intelligentsia were suspect. She was alone with her three small children. My presence endangered her and her children, but because of her love and loyalty for my mother, and her history of helping others, she took me in and sent her own children to the countryside with a nanny. I had survived by some miracle, but I had no idea how to continue, where to go, what was a safe haven. I did not speak for a week, so shocked and numb I was.*

# 7

# **Zosia Pozniak**

In 1978, my parents heard that Zosia Pozniak, the woman who had helped save my mother during the war, and who was still living in Krakow, had been invited for an audience with the newly-ordained Pope John Paul II. She and her family had been attentive and helpful to the Pope many years before when he was a young actor convalescing after he had been knocked unconscious by a German tank. When a woman picked him up, he asked to be brought to Zosia's home, and there he stayed while healing. He had never forgotten her kindness to him. It was extremely difficult to get a visa and passport out of Poland, but now that Zosia had the necessary travel documents offered by the Vatican, my father was able to arrange for her to continue on from Rome to Israel where at last she could be awarded the title of Righteous Gentile at Yad Vashem, a museum and monument in Jerusalem. Over the years, my parents had been sending her packages of clothing and treats over the years. Now it was possible to have her publicly honored. A ceremony was planned at Yad Vashem, where a tree would be planted in her honor along the Avenue of the Righteous Gentiles. She made the trip with many unexpected adventures, and was awarded a medal at a very moving tree-planting ceremony. As we were making plans for Mrs. Pozniak's travel, my mother spoke again.

## 1942 - My Piano Teacher Saved My Life

*While I was hiding out at Zosia Pozniak's home, a young man who knew me from Wieliczka and was one of the few, who, like me, had escaped the transport, came looking to see if I had made it back to Krakow alive. He knew to look for me at Mrs. Pozniak's home. I don't remember his name, but he was instrumental in helping me get to the next stage in my journey of survival. When he arrived, we all had a serious discussion about what to do next. Zosia reasoned that I should go to another city far from Krakow, where no one would recognize me. She suggested that he and I go together to Lwow (Lemberg), where her husband's colleague, Professor Banach, lived. Somehow she arranged to obtain a set of false identity papers for me, as Krystyna Banach. This name would make me appear to be a Christian girl related to this professor. Zosia also obtained 300 zloty from my father's store, from our loyal employee who still was working there, and managed to take the money from the cash register to give to me.*

*We took Zosia's advice, and the young man and I traveled by train to Lwow. When we rang the bell at the address given us by Zosia, a very pale and frightened Mrs. Banach answered the door. She stammered that she couldn't help us. Her husband had just been released from prison, along with other professors who had been held and interrogated, and she was too frightened to endanger herself and her children at such an unsafe time by taking in two Jewish refugees. The young man sat me in a nearby doorway while he went to find some other safe place to stay. I felt hungry and sick, just waiting. He returned after a long time, around midnight, and breathlessly told me that a policeman had stopped him and made him drop his pants. Discovered as Jewish, since only Jews are circumcised in Poland, he had promised to give the policeman money as a bribe to let him go. I gave him the remaining 300 zloty from the money that Zosia had given me, which he immediately handed over to the policeman. He found some friends to put us up for the night in their basement. The next day he went alone to get some food. He then left for the eastern front, where workers were needed and few questions were asked. I was all alone in a strange city. No job. No place to stay. No money. I have no idea what happened to him after that. I hope he survived.*

*While we had been living in the village of Wieliczka, my mother Mala had left a trunk of clothes with a peasant woman who had three daughters. Now I needed those clothes, and sent word to that village woman to please send some to me. But all she sent were a light evening dress and some flimsy shoes. With this I had to go to work in an office! The sewing class I had taken in 1938 came in very handy now. I was able to make a blouse and skirt from a curtain and tablecloth, which I dyed and sewed into something suitable for office work.*

*I got work immediately. The German I had learned in school, in order to en- joy poetry, and the increased fluency I had gained in my year in Vienna, now literally saved my life! I had a skill that was needed, since not many Polish people could speak and type in German. I applied for work in the office of a grocery store and was hired right away, when the owner was not there. I tried to blend in, be invisible, not be noticed, but I did not succeed. A German man named Karl came in and looked at me. He kept observing me and trying to engage me in conversation. The next day, the person who had taken over the store from the original Jewish owners and was now the German "owner" of the store came in, not knowing that I had been hired. He and I stared at each other. What kind of bad luck was this? He recognized me from the party at my Uncle Monek's house to which I had been invited a few years earlier. He knew exactly who I was, Monek's Jewish niece Bronia from Krakow. What an awful coincidence! He said not a word to me, but just wrote out a pink slip, which an employee handed to me. I was fired.*

*Karl, the German who had been hanging around the day before, saw that I was being fired, and must have asked the owner why. So now he, too, knew the truth about my identity. As I left the store in a daze, he waited for me outside. Now where do I go? I was emotionally empty, exhausted from the constant running, hiding, and trying to find a way to survive this night-mare.*

*Karl said to me quietly, "You are Jewish." I answered, "yes." I just didn't care anymore. I thought I was about to die. What was the point of resisting? He took me home and cared for me. I was still a virgin, but had no choice but to submit. So that was my introduction to sex, at age 22. I felt nothing. The will to survive is strong. Soon he was sent to the front, and I was again alone.*

*I soon found another job, working in a government tax office, called Izba-karbowa. Since this was a large office, I thought here I would be safer than before. But my safety there did not last long. I was still living under the as-sumed name of Krystyna Banach. One day a Polish man came up to my desk and said, "You are Bronia Kohn from Krakow." How did he know? He mentioned a woman, who was also Jewish with false papers, and who had come to this office. She somehow knew who I was and had pleaded with me to find her a job. I had said that I'd check, but there truly was nothing. She had informed on me. I had nothing much of value, only a small ring my mother had given me, at my high school graduation of the Hilfstein Hebrew Gymna-*

*zium. My mother had been so proud that I had finished with Matura (high level exams) in Polish and Hebrew subjects. What could I do? I handed the ring to him. He let me go, but since he knew who I was, I couldn't go back to that job. I found yet another job in an office. Again, my knowledge of German was put to an unintended use that saved my life.*

*There were informers - Ukrainian, Poles, and others - who could observe and identify people. They walked up and down the streets, working with SS in teams to seek out Jews who might have escaped the transports. One woman who was helping finger and identify people recognized me probably from Krakow, and I was arrested. They searched and found a letter from my father that I had hidden in my shoe, but apparently not well enough. They locked me up in a rat-infested jail with a drunken jailer who tried to rape me. I cried out that I had my period and somehow that kept him away from me. After two days I was called upstairs to the jail office. At the time I was captured, I had told the Ukrainian man, one of the informers, to let my boss know where I was being held. Thank God, he did get word to my boss where I was. My Aunt Bella's brother Arek, together with my boss, managed to give the huge sum of 50,000 zloty to the girlfriend of the SS man in charge of the jail.*

*Once I was released, I called my boss to thank him. He said, "Quickly, today, go by train to a place where no one knows you -- maybe Warsaw." Again, I lost my few possessions, and leapt into the unknown.*

*I went to the train station and boarded the train. I had no ticket and very little money. During the entire trip I pretended to be asleep. At every station, conductors and SS officers checked every passenger. Amazingly, no one woke me up or disturbed me, and I traveled straight through to Warsaw. It was another miracle.*

# 8

# Telephone Numbers and Addresses

I have a very good memory for telephone numbers and addresses. One time I was rattling off the numbers of my friends, along with their addresses, as a kind of joke. My mother said, "That kind of memory can save your life."

### 1943 - Remember My Address

*As I was pretending to be asleep on the train to Warsaw in 1943, I tried to remember an incident from a year earlier. While I was still living in Lwow, I had passed on the street the daughter of a professor friend of ours from Krakow. She said quietly as she walked by, "My false name is M… My official job is announcing arrivals and departures at the train station in Warsaw, but I am part of the Underground. If you are ever in Warsaw and need help, here is my address." I remember clearly that she quickly whispered a street name and number. Now a year later, I was in this strange city of Warsaw. I never had set foot here and had no clue where to go. I did need to find her. I scraped up a few pennies I still had and got into a bicycle rickshaw. The driver told me that we had only about 15 minutes until curfew, and asked me for my destination. I said, "Just drive around."*

*I thought and thought, and desperately tried to remember that scene from a year before. I replayed it in my mind's eye: She passes me, makes eye contact, tells me her address at such and such a street in Warsaw..... What was it? What was it? And suddenly I remembered and told the driver. We arrived at her place just before curfew. When she let me in, she said to me, "Bronka (she called me by one of my nicknames from my original Polish name of Bronislawa - Bronia, Bronka, Bronika), come in. We can be raided at any time. We will have to sit up in chairs all night. And if you hear noise, run." But we were safe at least for that night. Another miracle.*

# 9

# People-Watching

My mother and I were sitting in the lobby of a hotel in Switzerland on one of our summer vacations. I was about 12 years old. Somehow when we were in Europe, my mother opened up a bit more about her memories. Perhaps internal doors opened up when we were in countries where French, German, and other languages were spoken. There was something about the Old-World style of architecture, and the mannerisms and style of Europeans that triggered in her memories of the Second World War. As we sat in the lobby, Mom told me to look at the people coming and going. She said, "You can tell so much about a person, not just by how they are dressed, but by a certain air about them, an aura. You can see if they are confident, hesitant, curious, nervous. Did you know that you can smell fear? Yes, there is definitely a way to tell if someone is afraid."

### 1943 - The Smell of Fear

*There I was in Warsaw. I needed a new identity, so I sold my coat to obtain documents, and took on a new identity: Maria Zylinska, a Catholic Polish* woman. *Again I needed to find work and a place to stay. But it wasn't so simple. First one had to stand in a very long line, just to obtain a permit to be able to apply for an apartment and a job. And specially-trained soldiers walked up and down that line observing everyone. They could tell if someone was afraid. They could sniff out Jews or anyone they thought shouldn't have a right to be there. I had to stand as if I was just like everyone else. I had to project an air that communicated I had a perfect right to live and work there. No flicker of fear!*

*I did get the paper that allowed me to look for a room. The apartment was at Sniadecki 12/3. I still remember that address! The landlady looked me over and said with an edge of warning in her voice, "I live with my old mother and don't want any trouble. You are not Jewish." She probably suspected that I was, but wanted to be officially correct and stay out of trouble. She had a maid, probably also Jewish, who was very kind to me and often left me some food. I stayed there until the Warsaw Uprising in 1944.*

*I found a job as a secretary at the Steinhagen and Stranski Pump Company outside the city. So now I had a place to live and a job, but no warm coat for the harsh winter. As it got to be later in autumn, and the weather grew colder, I went to the boss, Mr. Blumke, who was Volksdeutche, a Pole of German extraction. This lineage qualified him to be a director of a company. I said I could not continue to work there. He asked, "Why not?" I replied simply, "I have no coat." This probably tipped him off that I was Jewish and had somehow escaped with no resources, because who wouldn't have a coat for the harsh winter? He was aware of my predicament, but never let on if he knew. He merely lent me a coat from his wife until the firm had a coat made for me from some artificial material with a rabbit fur trim.*

*The pay was barely enough to cover the rent, so to eat and cover my other expenses, I taught English in the afternoons. I had to leave by 3 p.m. while everyone else in the factory stayed until 5 p.m. The new Polish/German owner was a generous man. Together with the real owner of factory, a Polish gentleman, he offered a driver to bring me home each afternoon where my four students waited for their lessons. My text was A Christmas Carol by Charles Dickens. I managed to stay a chapter ahead of my students. The other workers in the factory office must have been jealous of me and angry that I could leave early.*

*Who knows what is bad or what is good? What is a curse and what is a blessing? I was securely in the hands of fate and had no idea what lay ahead.*

# 10

## A Kosher Meal

How is it possible to have someone else's flashback? Well, I did. I guess from having heard my mother's stories in bits and pieces over the years, they had become part of my own memory store.

During the last year of my father Alfred's life, he could no longer breathe easily in the high altitude of San Miguel de Allende, Mexico, where my parents had spent the winter for about ten years. They swapped their town house for a condo in West Palm Beach, Florida, and moved there. About the same time, a Polish man Andrzej Kasprzak (Andrew Casper in English) sought asylum in America to get away from the Russians who were occupying Poland. My mother and father met Andrew swimming at the condo pool and invited him home, where they all spoke Polish and became good acquaintances. After my father died in 1984, Mom developed a close friendship with Andrew, an elegant Polish man who understood her. Although he was Catholic, he shared many of my mother's memories. His own father had been murdered in Auschwitz as a Polish nationalist resistor. Andrew and my mother spoke Polish with each other, enjoyed the same food and music, and somehow carried each other's stories in a way no born American could.

It was March of 1998, and I was to join my mother in Poland where she was spending a few months with Andrzej, her companion of about 14 years by that time. Although they both lived in Palm Beach, he still had property in Poland, a house and a small hotel, as well as a mountain cabin, which he visited every couple of years. My mother never thought she would ever set foot in Poland again, but now she was planning a trip to stay with him in the Carpathian Mountains, at his cabin. We decided that I should come for a visit, and my mother would travel to Krakow to meet me. Mamusia (diminutive in Polish, like "Mommy") and I were both excited at the prospect of her showing me where she had lived before the war.

(Once I arrived in Krakow I was surprised to see color and flowers, and hear music. I had always imagined the city to be all brown, like a spy thriller-style sepia-tinged movie. Dark, silent, very gloomy. Dangerous. But that reaction had not yet happened. At this moment I had only just walked onto the plane and was beginning the flight to Poland.)

The most direct flights from Los Angeles were on Lot Airlines, the Polish airline company, which offered a direct flight to Krakow, where my mother would meet me. As I entered the cabin and took a seat, I tried to understand snippets of conversations I heard in Polish. I found that I could actually translate what one little girl asked her mother, and I could decipher some of the written signs in Polish about safety belts and trays. Although I had never spoken in Polish with my mother when I was growing up, I had spent years overhearing her talk to my father in Polish and German, to her friends on the phone, and at home parties, so I had this store of passive vocabulary. After the plane gained height and began to level off, a young, blond, Polish flight attendant approached me, looked up at the seat number, then back at me, and asked, "Did you order a kosher meal?" Suddenly it seemed as though the plane and the passengers had disappeared. My heart began to race in fear, and I felt as though I was back in Warsaw in 1943 at that pump factory. I could hear my mother's voice retelling a story closely related to those words, "a kosher meal."

## 1943 - A Kosher Meal? Identity Discovered

*When I was living under the name of Maria Zylinska and working in the office of that pump factory outside Warsaw, the next disaster struck. The girls who worked there were jealous that I had permission to leave early. This was no privilege, but rather a necessity, since I had to teach English in the afternoons to supplement my income to have enough money for food. They must have found out that I was Jewish. I never knew who gave me away, but one afternoon before I was about to leave, my phone rang.*

*I remember that moment as if it were happening right now: I pick up the receiver and hear a voice ask, "Would you like a kosher meal?" There is giggling in the background. I am in immediate danger. I put down the phone, leave the office and know that I cannot return.*

*At first I thought this was terrible luck. What I didn't realize at that moment of despair was that the call actually saved my life, yet again. After the uprising in 1944, soon after this incident that forced me to leave the factory, it was completely bombed. I had survived by yet another miracle.*

Back in the airplane I, Alicia, came out of my reverie, and forced myself to realize that this moment was over 50 years later; I was safe. And I answered the Polish flight attendant's question: "Yes, thank you." She smiled as if it were the most natural request in the world, and handed me a wrapped kosher dinner.

# 11

## Underground in Paris

When I was studying in Paris in 1967-68, during my Junior Year Abroad program at Sarah Lawrence College, my mother visited me. I was excited to show her around Paris, and the quickest way was by Metro, the fast and inexpensive network of underground subways. At first, my mother resisted, saying she hated tunnels and going underground. But one day she relented, and came with me to explore. For the rest of her stay, however, we took taxis whenever possible. I didn't realize why she couldn't handle being in subways. Then she told me about the underground tunnels that connected all parts of the city of Warsaw during the war. Eventually, the Warsaw Uprising to free Warsaw from the Germans came, while the Russians were waiting across the Vistula River to march in. My mother described her vivid memory of those months leading up to the Warsaw Uprising.

### *1944 - Maze of Tunnels Underneath the City of Warsaw*

*I remained in Warsaw where my knowledge of German allowed me to find yet another job after I had to leave the pump factory. I was lucky to find a job*

# FROM MIRACLE TO MIRACLE

*right in the city. One day by chance, I met an old friend who was a medical student. He had a non-Jewish wife. She said that she had to move to the countryside; would I go with her husband the next day to pick up some necessities needed for the move? I went with him, but on the way shooting broke out. It was the Warsaw Uprising.*

*My friend and I quickly ducked into the shelter of a nearby doorway to avoid the shooting, and I said to the medical student, "Be careful! Don't stick your head out; you'll get shot." He laughed and answered, "While in the ghetto, I was shot through the neck and the bullet passed right through me. I was taken out of the ghetto as dead, but nothing touched me. So I'm charmed; I'm safe." At that instant he stuck out his head to see if we could move on, and was instantly shot and killed. So there I was, alone, standing and shivering in the doorway. A woman from the apartment building where I was sitting came and picked me up by the arm and said, "Come inside to my place. This shooting will take a long time." And so the next chapter started. I had to begin again from zero to figure out what to do and where to go. I never saw my apartment again. Young children had learned the maze of sewer passages and dug-out passageways that crisscrossed underneath Warsaw. They led people through the confusing subterranean web of tunnels wherever one needed to go. It was too dangerous to be above ground because of the constant bombing. To this day I have a horror of going underground.*

# 12

## The Birthday Party

We were planning my birthday party. I was in the sixth grade. My mother and I had gone to the library and picked out a children's play that we liked. All my friends would have costumes depicting different animals of the forest. We would rehearse and then put on the play in our living room for all the parents. As we cut out trees and leaves for the scenery backdrop to be tacked onto the mantelpiece, I asked her, "Mommy, what did you do for your birthdays when you were a little girl?" She stopped decorating, got that distant focus, and answered, "I don't remember a single birthday or a single gift, except one. It was during the war."

### 1944 - One Memorable Birthday

*One day during the Warsaw Uprising, May 27, 1944, I was in an office, and suddenly a young man who adored me, although he did not know who I really was, jumped in through the window with a piece of black bread and ham. It was the most glorious present I ever got. The people of Warsaw were starving. The Russians refused to let airplanes from the Free Polish Army drop food to the city besieged by German troops. The army represented the Polish Government in exile stationed in London, England.*

*Soon after, a woman accused me of being a spy. Why? I lived alone, I knew German. Whatever the reasons, the bosses fired me. To test my loyalty and to give me a chance to prove myself, they sent me to work in a hospital. We had to give injections and care for soldiers with amputated legs. We had to be very strong and do everything.*

*The Russian army was stationed across the Vistula River. The Poles wanted to liberate Warsaw themselves, so the Russians just waited and didn't help at all. They didn't permit food to be brought into Warsaw. The uprising lasted about two months.[3]*

# 13

# Nothing to Eat

"Mommy! There isn't anything to eat!" I whined as I stood in front of the open refrigerator. My mother walked into the kitchen, looked at the shelves filled with bowls of leftovers, and the makings of several new meals, and laughed. How ridiculous my teen-age complaining seemed to her.

### 1944 - Starved Out

*When you say you are hungry, and you look in the fridge, and say, "There's nothing to eat," it really isn't true. We have so much! You can always find something and make a meal. But back then, I tell you, in Warsaw during the Uprising, there was literally nothing at all to eat. The Germans wanted us to die of hunger. And the Russians, who had previously agreed to allow the Polish national forces to bring food from England, now reneged, so Warsaw was under siege, and finally had no choice. They had to surrender to the German forces. The Poles were too proud to allow others to liberate their city, their people. They felt, "What? Russians should liberate my city??!" Meanwhile, the Russian soldiers were laughing, "You Poles want to free Warsaw? Fine!"*

# FROM MIRACLE TO MIRACLE

*The Russian soldiers stood across the Vistula River and simply waited. They didn't permit the Allied planes to land, refuel, and deliver the food that was so desperately needed. Then afterwards, the Russians marched in, and had Poland under their thumb for 40 years, under Communism.*

*This is beyond reason. Wars have no sense. Who can figure this out?*

*During the fighting I was working as a nurse in the Red Cross hospital right in Warsaw. I still retained my identity of Maria Zylinska. As far as anyone knew, all the remaining Jews had died in the Warsaw ghetto, in an incredibly courageous resistance against the Nazis that had lasted for several weeks, but there were still thousands of Polish people living in bombed-out Warsaw and valiantly trying to hold out against the German army. Many parachutists were shot down, some German, others Russian. When the Germans were winning, the German wounded lay in the few available beds and the Russians were on the floor. When the Russians were winning, the Russians occupied the beds and the German wounded lay on the floor. We nurses had a ration of three lumps of sugar to keep us nourished for the whole night of hard work. We were bombed every night by the Germans. I slept in one bombed-out building after another, like a rat finding shelter, wherever I saw a half a bed or a bit of a roof still intact. All I had was a tiny carrying case with some personal things and a few pictures remaining of my family. I had no information about whether any of them might still be alive. I had no time to mourn or feel any emotion about our abrupt separation, and their probable death. All my energy went into surviving day by day. Finally it was clear we had to surrender to the Germans. They had starved us out.*

*I came out of the Red Cross Hospital together with a doctor. We held white flags of surrender. I was wearing my nurse's uniform and heavy men's work shoes with thick laces. The laces came untied, and as I stepped aside for a moment to retie them, the doctor with whom I had been walking stepped on a land mine and was instantly killed.*

*I witnessed the scene, turned around, and went back to find another doctor to hold the white flag. No feelings, no reaction on my part. Numbly, mechanically, I just continued on with the formality of surrendering.*

*The Germans immediately asked me to work as a nurse. "Come schwester (sister, or nurse), please work for us." In a split second I had to decide whether to stay and work for them, or go to a prisoner of war camp. I figured that it would be very dangerous to carry on with my false identity of Maria Zylinska in a hospital for the German army. At least as a captured prisoner in the POW camp, we would be governed by the protective rules of the Geneva Convention. So I, along with nearly two thousand women, was taken as a prisoner of war to a camp near Berlin, where I would serve as translator.[4]*

*As we were getting ready to board trains from Warsaw to the prisoner of war camp, an international photographer arrived to take pictures of how well we were being fed and treated. It was all a sham for the outside world. The lack of food and terrible treatment would soon begin. But somehow we prisoners found creative ways to help each other survive.*

*Every time it appeared as though there was absolutely no way out of the current danger, I felt I was speaking to my mother whose spirit accompanied me and protected me throughout the horrors and perils I constantly faced. Although during my childhood I had felt much closer to my athletic, fun father, and rarely spent much time with my serious mother who always worried so much about me, now in my time of great need, it was she who appeared to me, and watched over me like a guardian angel.*

# FROM MIRACLE TO MIRACLE

*At that camp were many men who hadn't seen a woman in several years. When these male prisoners heard that there were women housed close by, they organized a group to cut the wire fence and crawl through to reach the women's section of the camp. We were not safe! The authorities guarding the camp realized that we would have to be moved, and very soon!*

*I was taken on rounds to parts of the camp to translate information about the prisoners, and I was recognized. By a great coincidence, Janek Gruenspan, my childhood boyfriend from Krakow, who had written to my family at the beginning of the war, was being held in solitary confinement at that very camp. His friends recognized me from the artist's painting of my portrait that he had shown them. I was still using the name of Maria Zylinska, a Polish Catholic, and could not risk having my cover blown, even here in a camp. One man approached me and said in a low whisper, "You are Bronia Kohn from Krakow, and Janek is in this camp, in solitary confinement. We will find a way to tell him you are here." So Janek knew that I had survived. The two of us were not to meet again until 1946, when he arrived in New York right after the war. By that time he had taken the French name of Jean Gavin, and our reunion was not anything that we could have imagined.*

*Our entire group of women was soon transported to Oberlangen in Germany, near the Dutch border, and there began a new chapter of survival.*

# 14

# Soup

When I was about ten, my mother served some homemade soup, with meat on the bone and vegetables. It still contained some fat floating on the top. The next day after it got cold, my mother would be able to skim the fat off, but for dinner it still retained some shiny globules. "Ew, ugh, I hate the fat. I don't want to eat that!" I exclaimed, making a less-than-polite face. My mother gave a strange half-smile, and replied softly, "Do you know what we would have given to have a tiny piece of fat in our soup, when we were in the prisoner of war camp?" She sighed, and I got very still, waiting for the story.

### 1944 - Soup, Food, Barter

*Can you imagine….There was not a smidgen of fat anywhere! Yes, that's true. How did we get food in Oberlangen? We had only horrible soup. I don't want to know what was floating in it. And that was all. I was working in the office of the camp as a translator, and so I became the middle man. We got packages from the Red Cross, but what was in them? Choco-*

*late, coffee, cigarettes, things that nobody thinks about when they are truly hungry. However, the Russian prisoners didn't get any packages.[5] They were not under the terms of the Geneva Convention for prisoners of war. They were taken out of camp each day to work on German farms, since nearly all the able-bodied Germans had been sent to war. The camp was very near Aachen, an agrarian area near the Dutch border, and workers were needed in the fields. So every day, those Russian prisoners were taken to work on the farms, and at the end of each day they returned from the fields with carrots, potatoes, onions, cabbages. Somehow, they hid the food. We gave them Chanel #5 eau de cologne which they drank because there was alcohol in it, and they smelled like perfume, whooof! They wanted the goodies in our packages, so we gave them chocolate, coffee, cigarettes, and "alcohol," and they gave us fresh vegetables.*

*Thirty women were involved in this operation. I was in the office, the ex-change person. One was in the laundry, another was in the infirmary. Every one of the thirty worked somewhere else in the camp. The one in the laundry had a fire constantly going to heat water in a big, big oven.*

*It was here in the camp that I saw for the first time in my life a washing machine for clothes. At home in Krakow, when I was growing up, we had always had a maid who washed our clothes by hand. A woman who had one tooth came to our house, boiled water in a huge cauldron, then scrubbed and cleaned all our clothes by hand. That was her job.*

*Getting back to our food operation: That is how I still have my own teeth, because I had access to carrots and potatoes and fresh foods with vitamins. And did you know that if you take one precious egg, and beat it for half an hour, it becomes fluffed up.... so high! I don't remember if we ate it raw or cooked, but it had some volume and lasted a longer time. And the potato*

# SOUP

*tasted like heaven, plucked out of the coals of the fire. Sometimes the woman in the laundry room misjudged the time, so the potatoes were burnt to a crisp. But mostly she remembered and brought them back, and they were delicious. There was no meat, but at least we had some vegetables with necessary vitamins to keep up our strength.*

*I kept the exchange of food and goods going on constantly. It was vitally important for all of us to eat some kind of real food, even though the amounts were small. We had a bit of what we needed, and the Russian prisoners had what they liked. This went on for a year.[6]*

*And do you know, there were some women who had become pregnant before the uprising. The babies were born beautiful, while the mothers were a mess: all their strength went into the babies. There were still a few very old men, Germans who were still at home, not fit for the army, who acted in a kind and humane way, and brought milk from their cows for the babies. The mothers didn't have enough food to produce milk. This is how we adapted to the difficult situation and somehow managed to survive. Inside the camp we didn't have any connection with the few remaining Germans in the surrounding farms, or any access to the outside world.*

*It was very cold. We had to crush ice in a bowl to wash ourselves. Our beds were thin straw mattresses on a double deck of wood planks. We slept two on a bed, head to toe, so we could share a thin blanket and stay warmer. It annoyed everyone how soundly I could sleep even under such conditions. One morning I awoke to find myself all covered with straw as a prank by my roommates! One finds ways to laugh even under very difficult circumstances.*

*Despite the supplement of some potatoes and vegetables, I was malnourished, yet bloated as often happens with an inadequate diet. I was 24, and deter-*

mined to survive to see how this whole insane drama would end. One part of me was watching, while another part of me was living. And as I was observing, I thought, "I don't believe what I see. This is not possible. Human beings cannot be so stupid, so cruel." And yet they are.

# 15

## Drug Education

I came home from high school and said that we had learned about the dangers of taking drugs. My mother looked off in the distance, beyond the living room walls, and sighed. "I never knew anything about drugs, until one day in the prisoner of war camp, I saw a woman on her knees rocking and acting very strangely."

### 1944-1945 - Prisoner of War Camp.

*Someone told me that the woman on the floor, rocking back and forth, had taken some drugs to numb herself from the pain and terror. It turned out that in order to have something to trade for the drugs, she had stolen my potatoes. She also took a small leather attaché case that I had hidden; it contained the only remaining pictures of my family. She didn't care about those and probably threw them out. How could she have known how very precious those pictures were to me?!*

*Under pressure some people break, while others find incredible strength and do not crack.*

# FROM MIRACLE TO MIRACLE

*About 30 of us were sent to Berlin, where there was bombing every day. We were pressured to sign papers saying that we would be civilians. But as prisoners of war under the Geneva Convention, we had at least some minimal protection and rights. The Germans forced us to walk through wind and snow and rain. We had to carry heavy mattresses filled with lice. We were exhausted, and so they cajoled us with promises, gave us white rolls, and offered better food, if only we would sign and give up our rights. Still no one signed. Angry and frustrated, the German officers barked, "Now all of you pack up!" and pushed us onto a train. We had no idea where we were being sent. I had an excellent memory and as I watched the countryside roll by the moving train, I called out to the others, "We are going back to our camp!" Such a reception we got! No one thought they would ever see us again.* [7]

# 16

## Love Letters in the Attic

When I was 16, I was looking through some dolls, childhood mementoes, and ballet costumes in the attic, where they had been stored. My mother came in and sat down on the floor with me, and started to rummage through an old valise. She cried out, "Oh look at all these old letters. I didn't know they were still here!" And she started to pull out packets of letters on thin paper, in beautiful handwriting, some written in English, some in Polish, one pile in red ink, others in blue or black. She said, with a sigh, "So many men were in love and wanted to marry me." I never peeked even at the ones I would have been able to read. But now as I work on the book and remind her of those packets of love letters, she laughs and tells me more details.

### 1944-1945 - Love Letters

*One packet of letters was from John Gibbs, an English officer who met me when I came to the prisoner of war camp near Berlin, along with nearly two thousand women soldiers immediately after the Warsaw uprising. They had to prepare documents for everyone and needed a translator to ask questions in German, Polish and French, and then translate them to English. John took me around the camp areas, wherever he needed translating done. The women were in immediate danger from the men in the other part of camp, men who hadn't seen women in several years. We had to be moved farther away quickly. We were taken to Oberlangen in Germany, near the Dutch border.*

*When I left, John Gibbs, the English officer, continued to write, and addressed me as "Maria." Our correspondence back and forth helped raise morale not only for me, but for my 30 roommates in the P.O.W. camp where we spent the last six months of the war in late 1944 and early 1945.*

*Another packet was in Polish. These letters were from Janek. He and the other prisoners were permitted to write a letter once a month. We received sporadic letters from him. I am sure that the very act of writing helped keep alive his hope that there would be a future after the horrors and deprivation of the war.*

# 17

# President Roosevelt

I loved to play *Men of Destiny*, a board game about the American Presidents, with my good friend Nancy Wallace. At the time we were probably about eleven years old. After an afternoon of play, I walked home, and told my mother that I was learning many interesting details about the lives of our American presidents. She said to me: "I know one important date about President Franklin D. Roosevelt! The day he died was April 12, 1945. That was the day I was liberated from prisoner of war camp."

### 1945 - Liberation

*It was the 12th of April 1945, the day Roosevelt died. Canadian and Polish forces had heard that there were over a thousand women in a camp out in the woods. So they came to check, and there we were, somewhere near the border between Germany and Holland. Polish forces of General Maczek's First Armoured Division marched in, along with Canadian soldiers. After they entered the camp to liberate us, I was summoned to assist them, since I was the translator for everyone. I was in the office and the other prisoner-workers called me, "Maria, Maria, come help." I was bewildered, not able to feel anything. I wondered what would happen next.*

*As the liberating officers began to make sense of who had been in charge of the camp, they questioned me to find out how the head of the camp had behaved. He was a sadistic German who had often amused himself by shooting over our heads after breakfast just for fun, and we had to lie down flat suddenly. So when the liberating officers asked me about him, I told them truthfully that he was a horrible, cruel monster. They shot him in front of me as I stood there. Human life came to mean zero.*

*A Canadian officer took me aside. My name was still Maria Zylinska, and that is how he addressed me: "Maria, I want to teach you two songs, and then you will sing them to the officers later when we have a dinner and a party." I knew practical English well enough but I didn't exactly understand the songs. In any case, I learned them by heart. One was "You'll Never Know" and the other one is "If I had my Way." Here are the lyrics, which I remember to this day, of "You'll Never Know":*

> *You'll never know just how much I love you./ You'll never know just how much I care./ And if I tried I still couldn't hide my love for you,/ You ought to know for haven't\* I told you so a million or more times?/ You went away and my heart went with you / I speak your name in my every phrase./ If there is some other way to prove that I love you,/ I swear I don't know how. / You'll never know if you don't know now."*

*That very evening I sang this song to hundreds of officers as they were eating dinner. How unreal, to be a prisoner one day, and free, singing a song the next. It was truly a memorable moment.*

*The liberators wanted to give us treats — sausage, sardines, heavy food, good stuff - but it was a dangerous thing to do. We hadn't eaten really for a year. The kind soldiers weren't nutritionists!! They should have given us just a little rice or cereal so we could get used to regular food slowly. We stuffed ourselves with the solid, heavy food, and became deathly ill. You couldn't find anybody walking around in the camp; they were all so sick right away.*

*I remembered what my childhood friend Janek had told me at the beginning of the war, about someone to contact in America if any of us survived the war. I asked a Canadian colonel in the liberating forces to send a letter to the orchestra conductor Rodzinski in NY. He did take the letter. Already in the early days of the war, I had heard that my aunt Ruth Bierman Licht, sister of my mother, and her husband Arnold had found refuge first in Paris, then in Holland, and through Panama, had finally immigrated to the States, and had settled in New York. I still didn't know if any of my immediate family, or my other aunts, uncles, or cousins who had stayed in Europe had survived. There was still no way to send a letter within Europe. It was all so chaotic. Now I was free, but I wondered, "Where should I go? Shall I stay Catholic? Go back to Poland?" I waited to hear any response from America, if my aunt and uncle could be located.*

*A funny adventure happened immediately after liberation. I still hadn't yet heard if my aunt and uncle in America had received the letter I had written. I didn't want to be exposed as not being who I said I had been for these past years, so I still held on to my false identity. The real cousin of the actual Maria Zylinksa was a major in the Polish Free Forces in London. He saw my name on a long list of liberated Polish women, and flew to our camp in Oberlangen to take me with him. Who knew where to turn or what to do? I was warned about his coming and went into hiding, since I knew the major would immediately recognize me as an impostor. Major Zylinski had to fly back to London without his cousin Maria. Before he arrived he had sent me shoes size 5. Maria must have had small feet. I had a size 8.*

*Slowly we began to get organized. There were many thousands of people displaced all over Europe. The Allied forces divided Germany into zones of influence - British, American, and Russian. American and British head-quarters in various cities throughout Europe tried to repatriate people or locate relatives in other countries to find the refugees a new home. So I had survived to see the end of the fighting, but now a new phase of my life began. I asked myself what to do now? How could I regain my real name and identity? Where could I go? Who had survived? Was there anyone alive from my immediate family? It would take months for me to find my own answers to these questions, but in the meantime, I was busy helping others reunite with their families and figure out the next steps in their journeys.*

*Because of my mother's slightly British accent, it was not until I actually looked up the lyrics for this chapter that I realized the word was "Haven't I told you so?" rather than "Heavens, I've told you so!" as I had heard it from her, and had sung it that way since I was a child!

# 18

## In American Uniform

As a young teenager in Highland Junior High School, in White Plains, N.Y., I was looking through our family photo albums, and came across a newspaper article showing my mother disembarking from the ship S.S. Richardson on Valentine's Day 1946. She was waving her hand, and was dressed in an American uniform. I asked, "Mom, how did you come to have an American uniform? I don't understand what you did while you were waiting to come to America, after the war was over." She looked at the picture and answered, "That was all I had, a khaki uniform from head to toe, since I had been working for the Americans as a translator for the G-2 department, in intelligence."

I interrupted, "Wait, Mommy, tell me more. How did you get to be working for the Americans if you were liberated by Canadian and Polish armed forces, and then worked as a translator for the British at various DP camps?" "Ah, that was a whole other adventure!" She smiled as she pointed to the documents next to the picture. I settled in for the rest of the story.

# FROM MIRACLE TO MIRACLE

## *1945 - Useful In Uniform*

*In order to go to America I had to get my original name back, and go to the American zone, for travel documents and passage to the United States, but at first after liberation I was working in the British zone.[8]*

*There is no picture of me in a British uniform; nobody took a photo. Who thought to take pictures? Every morning the general arrived with a chauffeur, and we traveled around the British zone of the German countryside in a car with the British flag flying. Because I spoke English, Polish, German, and French, we traveled to all the DP (Displaced Persons) camps. I spoke to all the people there in their own language. "Where are you from? Where do you want to go? What names of relatives are you looking for?" The people we interviewed were very grateful that I spoke their language, and could document their replies. People were searching for relatives, and putting their names on lists of survivors.*

*It was a time of confusion. Slowly I, too, was piecing together the fragments of who I was, and attempting to stitch them into a new person that I was becoming.*

*As I was doing this work, I thought, "Pinch me, this is unbelievable. I have no real name, no relatives, and no future that I can see. I'm just living day to day in this elegance, with attention and food. Suddenly not only am I safe, but also valued as a human being!" The British officers were segregated according to class, and I was placed in the highest level of the six they had. A kilted adjutant from Dublin was assigned to bring me to the officers' mess with the very top-ranking officers and eat dinner every night. What a leap - from my straw bed in the prisoner of war camp, to this!*

# IN AMERICAN UNIFORM

*Eric Langford Brook fell in love with me. He was the official liaison between the Polish and British forces. Many of the officers were in love with me, but I stayed away from any involvement, and was protected and guarded. I give myself a star that I held out, and told myself that I had to wait to make any major decisions until I got to America. I said to myself, "I want to marry a Jewish man when I am really free somewhere, not just floating like this." And I had to worry about the adjutant in the kilt -- he was supposed to be protecting me -- more than I worried about the people who might accost me somewhere else!*

*One of those officers was a lawyer with whom I corresponded for many years after the war. He wrote that he and his buddies got together every year and raised a toast "to Maria!" They met in London on the anniversary of liberation every April 12ᵗʰ.*

*After a while, a response finally came that the orchestra conductor in New York had forwarded my letter to HIAS, The Hebrew Immigration Aid Society, which helped settle Jewish displaced persons and reunite family members.*

*HIAS confirmed that Ruth and Arnold Licht were living in New York. Although I hadn't seen my aunt and uncle in years, I described them as well as I could, and the volunteers of HIAS located them in Forest Hills, Long Island. Although my aunt and uncle didn't even recognize my picture from the prisoner of war camp, they sent an affidavit that I should join them. So instead of going to Palestine, as Israel was called before 1948, where several of my friends who survived ended up, it turned out that I was destined to begin my life anew in America.*

*I found out years later that they had lost their property and houses in East*

# FROM MIRACLE TO MIRACLE

*Berlin, and had found their way to America with very little money. Their son Fred had been sent out of Germany as a young teenager. All by himself, he had traveled to South America, where he had to take care of himself for several years until he was able to rejoin his parents. His odyssey deserves a whole book. I had adored him, and took him to a local sweet shop in Krakow when his parents visited our home in 1932 when I was 12 and he was just five years old. Now I would be reunited with him at his parents' home! After his university studies he became an incredible linguist, art historian, professor and curator, specializing in Renaissance and Baroque art.*

*Uncle Arnold was working hard, carrying heavy suitcases of samples as a door-to-door salesman. Nevertheless, my aunt and uncle took a larger apartment with an extra room so that I shouldn't feel that I wasn't wanted and had to sleep in the kitchen. They wanted to make me feel welcome.*

*They generously sent me $500, which was an enormous sum of money in America at that time. But it went so quickly in post-war Europe, where money had no value.*

*Uncle Arnold gave me practical advice, and wrote, "You must go to Belgium to Monsieur and Madame Dineur, my business friends from before the war, and they will vouch for you, because you have no papers. Go to the Polish consulate in Antwerp, and make a declaration of your true birth name. They will issue you a passport so you can come to us in America. Then you must get a visa from the Americans so you will be allowed to immigrate to the United States."*

*Finding these relatives and having this invitation from them to start a new life seemed like a miracle. But there were several hurdles still to overcome.*

# IN AMERICAN UNIFORM

Can you imagine my mother's joy when her first grandchild, my daughter Avital (Tali) Magal was born on that date, April 12, years later in 1976?! My daughter's date of birth has incredible significance, since it represents that day of liberation, after which a new family would be created. My mother is now matriarch of the family, with two children and five grandchildren! We are all alive because of the miracle of her survival.

# 19

## Fashion Drawing

In an art class in White Plains, N.Y., High School, I had an assignment to copy a series of fashions from different eras. I showed my mother what I was doing, and asked her advice about how to draw folds and pleats, and how to shade different kinds of fabrics. By this time she had become an accomplished artist in oils, watercolors, pastels, and other media. She held the colored pencil in the air for a moment, gazed out the window and said pensively, "Drawing fashions, copying them from a stylish shop window, was my very first job, how I made a few dollars right after the war, and found out I had some talent in art."

### *Documents, Drawings, and Delays*

*Once I had made contact with my aunt and uncle in America, the British officers told me, "Now you have to be in the American sector, so that you can be transported to America." I had to find a Polish consulate, and there was one in Antwerp, Belgium. Several British liaison officers gave me personal contacts in nearby Brussels, so that I would have a place to stay while waiting for the documents to be processed.*

*I went to my boss, who gave me a car and driver because one couldn't travel freely through Europe. It was still dangerous.*

*I arrived at the Polish consulate in Antwerp, Belgium. I was able to prove with the help of the Dineurs as witnesses, who had known my family before the war, that I was Bronislawa Felicia Kohn. Finally, I could give up my false identity as the Polish Catholic woman Maria Zylinska. From then on I chose to be called "Nika," a short version of my nickname Bronika.*

*I had incredible good luck in my timing! The document confirming that my real name was Bronislawa Felicia Kohn and a Polish passport containing that name and my real birth date were issued on the 26th of September, 1945. The very next day, the Communists took over power in Poland; the consulate became Communist, and stopped issuing passports. I would not have received my papers. Another miracle in my journey. If I had waited another day, I would have been stuck with no way to leave Europe.*

*While in Belgium, I had to stay somewhere, so I called upon the British officers' relatives, whose addresses had been given to me. One contact was an officer's aunt, a Madame Witouk. Her home was like a palace with huge gates, very elegant. Only a few weeks before, I had slept on straw in a prisoner of war camp, and now I entered a mansion. The jump from one extreme to the other was shocking. After the POW camp, I was showered with sudden elegance: breakfast on a tray with a rose, a bathtub with golden lions' legs. Despite the luxury, I stayed with her for only two nights, because she had strict rules about being home by 8 p.m. or the gate was locked and the servants went to bed. It was too formal and restrictive for me. I wanted to explore and feel free! It was so heady to be suddenly all on my own. It was like a dream.*

*I lived day to day, still not quite believing that I was free. There was still no way to get any news, but I had little hope of seeing any of my family alive. I focused on getting to America.*

*I needed a place to stay, and contacted the wife of Mr. Mersh, a liaison officer I had met. This wonderful woman, Simone Mersh, who lived in Boisfort, a suburb of Brussels, was so warm and kind to me that I came to call her "My Belgian Mommy." Imagine what it meant to me when she told her own son, "Maria gets the white rolls. They are not for you, because she has suffered." I had not yet changed my name, so that was still how I was called. We kept up contact through letters and visits after the war for many years. I'll never forget her kindness and warmth, which I needed as much as food and shelter.*

*I stayed at her home while I was waiting for my passport with my new name and all the other documents to be prepared. Simone Mersh's mother had a clothing factory in Brussels. The mother asked me if I could draw, and would I copy clothes from an elegant boutique. She then could have them sewn. I passed by the elegant store on the main street in Brussels that she indicated, with highly-styled designs and flowing fabrics. I did the drawings, and found that fashion design and drawing came easily to me. That was my first art adventure. I had the idea that maybe I would become a dress designer when I came to the States.*

*The $500 my aunt and uncle had sent me were spent in three days. I needed shoes and other necessities. Nobody wanted money; they wanted barter, real supplies. So now I was "free," but had nowhere to go and no money. Once I got my papers, I thought, "Ah, now I can regain my identity and* *start the next part of my journey." But even though I now had a passport and a visa with my name of Bronislawa Kohn, there was no transport to the U.S. for perhaps six months, until the American troops were shipped back home. I found a Jewish officer, who was a Second Lieutenant at the American headquarters in Antwerp, and explained my plight. He asked me to wait a day, and when I returned the next day, he had a plan. "You speak some French, right?" I nodded. "OK, we have an order for 39 Belgian girls to work in the Allied sector in Intelligence. So here's what we will do. You will go with this group of Belgian women to Frankfurt and work there, and wait for a transport. So, you are now a Belgian civilian working for the Americans in G-2, gathering information for the Counter-Intelligence Corps. You will have the rank of lieutenant. We'll call you back here when it is time to return and there is a ship available." I still have that document, dated October 22, 1945. It states that "Bronislawa Felicia Kohn, formerly known as Maria Zylinska, has the permission of the Supreme Commander Allied Expeditionary Force to enter the Zone of the Allied Forces in Allied Occupied Germany,"*

*I had just come from Germany to Belgium, and couldn't imagine that now I had to go back to Germany to wait for months until I could finally travel to the U.S.! The American officers issued me an American uniform and sent me to Frankfurt, which had been bombed to rubble. It looked like miles of chimneys. The city had been completely razed, except for IG Farben Industries, which the Americans used as a post-war administrative headquarters, and the Kronberg Castle, where we went for weekend relaxation. It looked like heaven to me, but there still was no communication with the outer world. In a strange way, it was a pleasant time to recuperate from my ordeals and begin to think, trust, and feel human again.*

*Many years later, in the 1990's, I returned to the Kronberg Castle with my companion Andrew. We had high tea, which was out of this world. I told the tour guides where everything had been immediately after the war. Andrew and I were royally treated on a special private tour. But you have to remember from what I came into what… from a pauper to a palace!*

# 20

## Sixth Sense; She Just *Knew.*

My mother just "knew" things, and we even counted on her intuition. One day when my brother Willy and I were in elementary school, we were riding home when the chain on Willy's bike broke. We couldn't get the bike to move. We sat by the road and sent a thought wave: "Mommy, come. Mommy, come. Mommy, come." I was about to ride home by myself and get her to drive back and pick up Willy and his bike. Then, to our amazement, she appeared, and asked worriedly, "What happened? I sensed something was wrong." When I later asked her how she just "knew things," she got that look, and told me this story. I have heard it several times, but never could grasp how she made so many life-changing decisions, based on nothing more than a strong intuitive knowing.

### *1945-46 - I Just Knew It Was Time to Go*

*While I was waiting for transportation to the United States, I had to support myself. I was given the rank of Lieutenant, wore an American uniform, and was headquartered in Frankfurt where I worked with the Belgian young women in the office. I was marking time, waiting for the call to return to Belgium.*

*The officers in charge of transport from the American authorities in Belgium had said to me, "We'll call you." But in late December, I said, "I must go." The American colonel in Frankfurt replied logically, "But they didn't send for you yet. You'll have to wait." I countered stubbornly, "I feel I must go, now. It must be right." The American Command gave the release and offered me a chauffeur and limousine, because it was still dangerous to travel in Europe alone; people of every nationality were roaming, searching, traveling in every direction. A Restricted Directive from December 26, 1945 lists me as Bronislawa Kohn, Belgian civilian attached to Counter-Intelligence Corps, who has "permission to proceed from her present station about December 28 to Brussels by military vehicle. The cost of transportation will be borne by the U.S. War Department... by command of General McNarney."*

*When I arrived at the American Consulate in Antwerp, the clerks looked at me in shock and said, "We just called the Frankfurt headquarters and you weren't there. The officers said you had left. How did you know to come now?" It's true. Exactly while I was traveling, they had called. That's when I realized I was psychic, and should always trust my feelings and intuition.*

*They issued a letter: "The Consulate General is pleased to inform you that it has received the allotment of one non-preference number for your use during the current month. Considering the short period during which this number may be used, it is of paramount importance that you call during the current week having in your possession two birth certificates, a valid travel document or passport, and three passport photographs taken with a white background*

# SIXTH SENSE; SHE JUST *KNEW*.

*on thin paper, front-view, and without a hat." The letter was signed by George Carnahan, American Vice Consul. It was now January, 1946.*

*I was ready and had my papers, but there still was no regular trans-Atlantic transportation. One ship was slated to bring war brides to the States, and I begged and pleaded to travel on that. I stood every morning waiting at the dock at 8 am. Ready. One day the transportation officer said, "I cannot stand to look at your face anymore. You are going on that ship, the S.S. Richardson, with the war brides." Soldiers had picked up these women, many of them common guttersnipes in Paris, in Belgium, everywhere. Few of them were truly the kind of wife material the men would have chosen back home. I wondered if those marriages would last. I was the only one who was not traveling to meet her American husband. I was still dressed in full American uniform and a leather jacket, since that's all I had.*

*We were finally ready to go. After three hours out of port, we got word that there was some technical problem and we had to return to shore; they had forgotten to load something. "I knew it's too good to be true." Where should I go now? So a woman with a child said, "We also have to come back in three days, so come with us," which I did. .*

*At last we took off from port. Soon we approached the Azores, with hot, tropical weather. After that, it was the end of good weather and smooth seas. I didn't believe we'd make it. Every day there was another storm, and the cutlery and plates were flying from side to side and smashing to the floor. For three long weeks everyone on board was sick. We lived mostly on crackers and apples. I couldn't deal with four women throwing up in hammocks below in the crowded cabin. I stayed up on deck most of the time. And I listened to Bing Crosby songs on an officer's record player. I learned every word of every record.*

# FROM MIRACLE TO MIRACLE

*One morning in February, as I stood on deck as usual, I saw something which wasn't endless water. I screamed "I see land!" It was the New York harbor skyline. There was great excitement, and then a let-down, when we learned that we could not land because there was a tugboat strike in New York harbor. We had to continue on to Philadelphia. I worried how my aunt and uncle would find me. I was elated, scared, worried, and hopeful, all at the same time. To my surprise, once we got to Philadelphia, they were the only two people waiting for passengers on the dock. It was February 14, a holiday in America. That Valentine's Day 1946 will always be my great personal holiday when my new life began. To this day I celebrate Valentine's Day as the anniversary of my arrival, the day of my new beginning.*

# 21

# Greetings After An Absence

I arrived home from camp, hugged my mother, and said how much I had missed her. On the ride home we heard commercials playing on the radio. I sang along. "N-E-S-T-L-E-S... Nestle's makes the very best.... Choc-late!" followed by a loud snap shut of my jaws. My mother laughed. "You take it as natural that there are commercials, and you think it is natural to get a hug when you come home."

## 1946 - First Commercial: I Am Chiquita Banana

*When I arrived in the United States after the war, I was all alone on a ship full of war brides. I was dressed only in the khaki American uniform I had from my months of work after liberation with the American Army Intelligence Corps as a translator. My uncle Arnold and aunt Ruth Licht met the ship which had been slowly making its way on a stormy ocean for three weeks from Belgium. A further delay was caused by a tugboat strike in New York, making it necessary for the ship to be detoured to the port in Philadelphia. After we sighted land, we heard on the radio my very first commercial, for*

# FROM MIRACLE TO MIRACLE

*Chiquita Bananas. "I am Chiquita Banana and I'm here to say, you must always treat bananas in a special way… You can put them in a salad, you can bake them in a pie-ie. Anyway you want to eat them, there is not a way to beat them. So remember that bananas come from very, very tropical equator. So you must never put bananas in the refrigerator… Oh no no no!"*

*We asked, "What's a commercial?" Everything felt so strange and new.*

*It was Thursday, February 14, 1946, Valentine's Day. I had never heard about this holiday, but it sounded like a lovely omen, a good day to land on the shores of a new country, with hopes of a safe, loving, new life. I was the first one off the ship, early as always. The local paper, The Philadelphia Evening Bulletin, wrote a story about me, and how I wanted to be a dress designer. The headline read, "Polish Girl, Heroine of Underground, Wants to Be a Dress Designer." I still have a copy. I came down the gangplank and there stood my uncle and aunt, Arnold and Ruth Licht. They had thought that I was dead, along with the rest of my family, and yet, here I was. What was the greeting, the homecoming, the reunion after those terrible years of fear and loss? My uncle smacked me on the behind with an umbrella and said in Polish, "Ty malpo"! "You monkey." It must have been to break the embarrassment, and to substitute for all their emotions at seeing me alive. I was the only survivor from my immediate family. Ruth was my mother's sister, one of eight sisters and four brothers. I lived with them in their Forest Hills apartment; they told me I could stay as long as I needed. What they didn't tell me and I didn't learn until many years later, was that at great expense, they had rented this larger home just to be able to give me my own room. All I wanted was a place of my own so that I could start a family. I stayed with them for only five weeks before I got married. But that is another story.*

## GREETINGS AFTER AN ABSENCE

No therapists could have understood or helped the survivors talk about their experiences. It would take another thirty years, perhaps in the 1970's, until psychologists and researchers began to explore and record the memoirs of the survivors.[9]

# 22

# How Did You Meet Your Husband?

At the age of 25, I left my job teaching French in the Weston Connecticut High School. Why? I loved teaching, and had been offered tenure; I cared about the students; I appreciated the department head and principal of the school; I had a state-of-the-art language lab at my disposal, and I enjoyed the modular, flexible schedule of the school day. I could easily have stayed.

One day, however, I looked at my hands, covered with yellow chalk and blue mimeograph ink, and thought, "At my age, my mother had survived a war and started a new life in the United States. The fact that I was born was a miracle. What have I done so far in my life? I've been a student and then became a teacher. What am I doing for my own people to justify my being alive?" Through an unusual series of events, just a few months after that transformational moment, I arrived in Israel, ready to begin a six-month "ulpan" work-study program at Kibbutz Maagan Michael, on the Mediterranean coast. Tired and hungry from the very long trip, I walked into the dining room late in the evening after everyone had already finished dinner. A young man was sitting at the table after having just completed the clean-up from dinner. I said, "I'm going to start the ulpan program tomorrow; I've just arrived, and I'm hungry." He smiled and said "I'll feed you." He offered me a huge and tasty selection of salads and cheeses, and some halvah, a sweet sesame paste dessert I'd never tasted before. I thought, "I'm going to like it here!" Little did I know that this handsome young kibbutznik, Itzhak Magal, the very first person I met on the kibbutz, would become my husband two years later, and that seven years later, we would return together to the United States, married, and with two children!

After I told this story to my mother's friends, who asked me how I had met my husband, my mother narrated her own story about how she met my father in the first few days of arriving in this country. We later expanded her story and included it in a booklet of personal Holocaust testimonies for Yom HaShoa (Holocaust Remembrance Day) at the Jewish Community of Sedona and the Verde Valley, where I have served as the rabbi since 2006.

## 1946 - How I Met My Husband

*The first day I arrived in Forest Hills, at the apartment of my Aunt Ruth and Uncle Arnold, there sat a man who introduced himself. He extended his hand to me saying "When I heard that Bronia Kohn was looking for Dr. and Mrs. Eder who lived in Krakow before the war, I knew exactly who this was. Mrs. Eder was knitting beautiful outfits for the Polish Pavilion of the World's Fair in 1939. I was taking a medical exam to get my American license, and a Dr. Eder was also taking his exam. He and I exchanged telephone numbers after the exam, and here it is. I hope this is helpful to you."*

*I called.*

*Here is an example of fate's humor. It would be hard to make up such a plot in fiction! At the very beginning of the war my mother Mala said, "I hear that you can be married by proxy. Write a letter and see if anyone will marry you by proxy, so you can get out of Poland." The Eders, who were already in America by then, living in New York after the World's Fair, had received our letter, and thought "What a naïve, silly thing to try to do." They had read it out loud to their friends, a group of refugees who were stuck in America at the outbreak of World War Two. Alfred Fleissig was there at the time they read the letter, and they all laughed about it then. Who would have the last laugh? You will hear!*

*Seven years later, here I was in New York. The Eders were dumbfounded to learn that I had survived. They threw a party for all the "Krakow refugees," among them Janek Gruenspan.*

*Janek, my childhood boyfriend, who had taken the name Jean Gavin, asked to see me alone and said, "After liberation I was sent to Paris. There I met a French woman who nursed me back to life when I was near death. I was a walking skeleton, weighing maybe 100 pounds. She was a sculptor, 15 years older than I. She helped me to survive, and I would like to marry her. Since you and I were unofficially engaged before the war, I decided I would not bring her over from Paris unless you first released me from our promise, and said this was OK." I answered, "You are free, and you must marry her; I am glad for you." He did bring her over, and they were married.*

# FROM MIRACLE TO MIRACLE

*Another of their friends in this circle was Alfred Fleissig. Like the Eders, Alfred Fleissig had come to the U.S. for the 1939 World's Fair. He had been sent as representative of a Polish cable factory. Once the war had broken out, he couldn't return home. He stayed in New York and worked as an engineer in the industrial firm of Hydropress. He spent the entire war trying to get his wife Selina and baby daughter Elizabeth out of Europe. The false Guatemalan passports he was able to acquire for them saved them for a time, but near the end of the war, all those with such passports had been rounded up and taken to concentration camps. Alfred was informed that his wife and child had been killed in Poland. Since he now knew that he was officially a widower, he was free to marry. Once he met me, he began to call me every morning at the same hour. I got used to his kindness and persistence. One week, he went away with a few friends and wrote a series of postcards in Polish, which translated as "Should we? The next one, "Could we?" and the last one, "Let's!"*

*I wanted to be safe and have my own home. I wanted time to heal from the crazy nightmare of the past seven years. I felt that with Alfred I could raise a family and slowly come back to being my own person again. Five weeks later I was married to this generous, protective, fatherly man, 14 years my senior. I basked in his love, and felt safe. I grew to love him, and always was grateful that he helped me heal from the unimaginable experiences and losses I had endured. How ironic! Alfred Fleissig had been present when my letter arrived at Dr. Eder's home, at the outset of the war, asking to find me a husband by proxy! They had laughed then at my naïve idea, but it was no fake proxy marriage that was about to take place, but a wedding for real! We were married on April 5, 1946, in Atlantic City, New Jersey. When Alicia, our first child, was born the following year, I said to this beautiful and serious little baby, "You have given me back my name." That is how I felt, that I was now really a person, because I was a mother. Four years later, I gave birth to our son William, and our family was complete.*

*Alfred and I were married for 38 happy years until he died in 1984. As I look back at the story of how I survived, and started a whole new life, I am amazed. It all seems like a dream filled with danger and adventures and a guardian angel watching over me, from one miracle to the next.*

# 23

## Intimate Stranger

In the late 1950's and early 1960's when my father had business in Europe, the family took the opportunity to travel to Europe, too. Daddy flew while my mother, brother, and I had the adventure of traveling across the Atlantic Ocean aboard the Statendam, an oceanliner of the Holland America line. Willy and I spent a few weeks in Gstaad, Switzerland, at a children's summer camp, a boarding school or "kinderheim" during the winter. Then, together with my mother, we traveled through Switzerland to Holland, and visited other countries.

I was ten, and we were on the train. I was walking back and forth down the corridor on one side of the train. I could see through the partially open door of our compartment that my mother was talking to a woman whom I had briefly met before going off to explore. Her name was Vera. They were facing each other with their legs stretched out on opposite sides of the banquettes. My mother's hand was covering her eyes, and by her lowered head and shaking shoulders, I could tell she was crying. In that instant,

## FROM MIRACLE TO MIRACLE

I knew, with a kind of compassionate jealousy, that she was revealing an Important Story to the Stranger. I was glad she had someone safe to talk to, but also sad and a bit resentful that I would not know that story, whatever it was. I never saw that lady again, but I'll never forget that scene.

(Originally written as a newsletter article for Temple Emanuel of Beverly Hills, California, in the mid-1990's; and then edited for a Yom HaShoa collection of personal stories presented at the Jewish Community of Sedona and the Verde Valley in 2007.)

# 24

# Reaching Back

(The following was originally written as a newsletter article for Temple Emanuel of Beverly Hills, California, in the mid-1990's; and then edited for a Yom HaShoa collection of personal stories presented at the Jewish Community of Sedona and the Verde Valley in 2007)

If you had fewer than five minutes to grab your most precious possessions before evacuating your home in case of, heaven forbid, fire or some other disaster, what would you carry to safety? Life is more important than any object, so we are not discussing children or animals; rather, those "things" we accumulate over a lifetime and enjoy having around, objects with personal meaning. I played this mental game as I carefully looked over cabinets and shelves of decorative mementos, books, albums, and ceremonial objects collected over 20 years of marriage, plus a few items from my childhood home. No contest at all: my matriarchal kiddush cup is my most treasured heirloom. It is my only tangible connection with my mother's family, who perished in the Holocaust.

# FROM MIRACLE TO MIRACLE

When I polish this small, stemless, silver cup, only 2 ½ inches tall, etched with designs of houses and trees in the typical Polish style of the 19ᵗʰ century, and the six slender matching cups that surround it, I wonder about my mother's mother Amalia, who kept these cups shiny more than 60 years ago in Krakow. The "A" of her name sparked the "A" of the Alicia that I became, in her memory. I cannot think of her as a grandmother, but simply as my mother's mother, because a grandmother is someone who hugs you and smiles with joy at how much you have grown, and the clever things you say as a child. I never felt her embrace or heard her gentle voice. As I rub the creamy silver polish, I wonder if by some magic, her reflection might appear in the cup's shiny memory.

How else can I reach back and touch the one who was "kind and good," fourth of eight sisters, the one who gave birth to the beautiful, sporty, independent one, my mother? "You are like her," I often heard as I was growing up. I felt proud, praised, but wished I knew it from observation and companionship, not merely from black-and-white photos taken before the war, and from other people's stories.

How to reach her? I take her name for the honored times when I am called up to the Torah by my Hebrew name, Ha-Rav Amalia bat Bracha (Rabbi Amalia daughter of Bracha, my mother's Hebrew name), and silently invite her to accompany me. She would be shy and unaccustomed to such ritual, impossible in her day before women were given such honor in the synagogue. Did she ever know the Hebrew meaning of AMALIA, "Worker of God"? Or was she content with her Jewish identity of MALKA, "Sabbath Queen," a gentler role, one nickname derived from her full name? I chant the words of our tradition and introduce myself at women's Rosh Hodesh (New Moon) celebrations as Amalia bat (daughter of) Bracha bat Amalia, tracing my maternal lineage, as my name repeats hers, and sense a fleeting generational link one I have always craved.

One day, this cup will be filled with wine at my daughter's Shabbat table, this women's cup, modest, womb-shaped, filled with the joy of life-giving. Our son has his own cup from his Bar Mitzvah. This one will not go to his household. For this mother-to-daughter cup, I will find a silver tray, and inscribe on it, "Amalia Bierman Kohn - Nika Kohn Fleissig - Alicia Fleissig Magal-Tali Magal ... followed by her married name which lies still in the mystery of the future for my daughter, who is just finding her wings, approaching the time of making her own nest. Now in 2009, I know the answer: My daughter is engaged to Craig Fleishman, and I am looking for a silver tray to engrave with our circle of mothers' names.

At my age, Amalia Bierman Kohn no longer drank from the cup of life, and this cup lay buried in the wartime soil, hidden, unheld for years. But metal can be retrieved and shined back to use. My mother's cousin Victor Johannes was able to locate the cup and return it to my mother after the war. Truly a miraculous treasure, representing an entire household of beautiful objects lost to us.

And Amalia? All I can do is wear her name and make peace with my reflection in her cup, as we bless wine and sing songs to welcome in that Malka - Shabbat Queen - who visits our home in our weekly Eden, where time dissolves and we can reach back.

# Postscript

I asked my mother over the phone, "Mamusia, what is the message that people should get after reading your book about surviving the war?"

*"Unfortunately," she answered, "people rarely learn from another person's experiences. If they do, it depends on what they are ready to hear. But OK, I'll write you an e-mail after I think about it a while. And when will you finally be done with this book?"*

I smiled, thinking about the long process of editing and researching that was still ahead. For my mother, it is so simple. She talked to me in person or on tape about her memories, and that was it. I had heard many of the stories before. Why couldn't I just write them all down quickly? Why wasn't I done yet? She couldn't understand. In telling me her story she rarely mentioned her feelings. She only said, "We were sent to the camp." Or, "I was left all alone." No emotions. I think I had been carrying her unexpressed feelings for many years, shadowed by the darkness she dared not explore. I never had clear boundaries. Even though in reality I had had a happy and safe childhood, on some level my mother's story was my story; my mother's loss was my loss.

Now in writing down her story, and asking some of the questions I never dared ask before, I am able to separate, and emerge as whole, with my own story to tell. In writing her memories, thoughts and experiences, I am releasing myself from the mystery of that cloud of sadness and loss that she never expressed.

Later, my mother wrote in response to my question about what she thinks people can learn from her experiences:

*I am thinking back on my life that started so happily: loving parents, adorable brother, an unusual gymnazium (high school) in Krakow- our graduation which included tough Matura exams, with four subjects in Hebrew, in additional to the regular exams in Polish like in all other schools.*

*I learned to walk straight and unafraid, from my non-Jewish neighborhood to the Jewish quarter, where my school established by D. Hilfstein was located. On Sundays most children were walking to their church while I was walking with my schoolbag on my back. You can imagine the looks I got. This ability to hold onto my own dignity in the face of animosity, turned out to be a great help, even a life-saving one. You have to know who you are, without all the trappings of position or family or money. You have to rely on your talents and skills which are all we really have. Everything else can be taken from us.*

*I learned to accept the fact that we were a minority in an almost 100% Catholic country. After 500 years, we were still completely segregated. Little did I know that beginning in 1939, events would change all our lives completely and make me an orphan. I would be left all alone, without money, clothes or friends. I had a strong constitution, and knowledge of four languages.*

*The lesson is that in such a time one learns "Who am I?" I survived such horrors because of my instincts. I had no one to ask advice and I hid under a false name. I had to be constantly vigilant and trusting no one.*

*There were a few nice, kind people. Without them no one could have survived.*

*One also has to be very, very lucky, and believe in a better future. I had this strong feeling - "I must survive to see this injustice avenged!" I think when our time is up, it is up. And if it is not, and you are meant to live, you will live. OK, you have to help a little.*

*I learned that one cannot generalize: I was once endangered by a nasty Jewish woman, who sent a policeman to arrest me to free herself. I met a number of Christians who saved my life when they could have turned away. So there are good people and bad ones. In tough times, one discovers the truth about people, and it has nothing to do with religion.*

*My survival was a combination of luck and determination - that is all. In order not to just hide and be afraid constantly, I worked in a Red Cross hospital. We got 3 lumps of sugar for the night duty and had to take care of soldiers who parachuted into Warsaw. Many of them became amputees. I spoke about how the Germans offered me a job as a nurse after they took over Warsaw, and how I had to make an instant decision. I thought that it would be better to be transported as a prisoner of war under the Geneva Convention than stay and possibly be recognized by someone and lose my life in Poland. All these decisions were taken in minutes, trusting my gut only.*

# FROM MIRACLE TO MIRACLE

*There is no blueprint for war or for liberation. You meet people in the raw. Everyone makes it all up, what to do next. And you ask yourself "Am I dreaming??" Usually we live with some boundaries, according to rules. You do this on Sunday, and you do this when company comes. But when war comes, everything is out the window and you just improvise, so that everybody behaves out of kilter.*

*Even in the bad times, especially dark, scary moments, never ever lose your sense of humor, and try to help others so that you forget your own troubles.*

*I am blessed with good health and I think I enjoy life now twice as much as any normal person. Things, objects, possessions mean very little to me. The challenge is to learn new things to appreciate every moment on this earth.*

*I am looking forward to celebrating my 90th birthday. I actually feel young and full of plans, even though I'm sitting in the body of an old woman. I love to dress up because you just never know what possibilities are waiting each day!*

*I am open to any adventure- nothing can stop me!!! In the last couple of years I had operations to get new parts - a hip and a knee. They were painful, but I met nice people in rehab and made two good friends. Enjoyment of life never stopped. I could have been bitter and angry, but that would have made it impossible to live. I would have been stuck back in wartime, even after liberation.*

*Such a colorful life I've had. Can you imagine that just a few years before the war, I had walked on the street in Krakow and asked myself, "Am I going to live my whole life here?" Two hours from Krakow, I traveled maybe once to see my aunt, and once to see my grandmother. And now in my 80's, I can*

# POSTSCRIPT

*look back on the years since the war, and delight in the fact that I've had wonderful adventures, raised a family, and traveled all over the world, including the North Pole. I could never have imagined the chapters that followed the war. They were so completely disconnected from my childhood.*

*Creating art and playing bridge helped me to get over "dark thoughts," which inevitably come uninvited.*

*My greatest blessings are my daughter Alicia, son William and five grand-children. Now I know why I survived!*

*Calusy* ("kisses" in Polish) *and never lose hope!!!!!!*

Email message July 12, 2010 from Nika "BrahaNika@earthlink.net" To children: Alicia Magal, Will Fleissig, and grandchildren: Tali Magal, Amir Magal, and David Ferrell.

*My Dearest children and grandchildren,*

*Woke up this early morning Monday with tears in my eyes and feeling of pain in my heart.*

*Tali's wedding (August 1, 2010 on Cape Cod) is almost here and that brought a feeling of transition. My time is over and yours is beginning.*

*Cannot give you much in worldly goods but am looking at the 3 remaining Venetian goblets\* brought by Zosia Pozniak after the war and with them is the memory of a good warm home, happy* *childhood, my beloved parents, Mala and Binciu, and brother Toldek - my whole happy world for 20 years.*

*Looking at these goblets which stood in our dining room I ask my-self why was I spared to suffer alone for so many years ?*

*You are the answer- I had to start a new family from the ashes of murdered innocent people- a few had to survive to continue our Jew-ish heritage.*

*Now I am beginning to understand why Alicia became a Rabbi - She will help all of you after I am gone to survive the normal (not always easy) life.*

*Always remember "we are special" and have to show others how to love- how to live and help others! This is what I am leaving in your hands and know that you will always remember!*

*With love always yours,*
*Mamusia Babcia Bronka (Nika)*


*Alicia adds: Zosia Pozniak came to visit our family in White Plains N.Y. in the 1960's and brought the glass goblets that had been given to her to keep by Nika's parents at the start of the war. Other than the silver Kiddush cup set, they are the only things Nika had from her childhood home in Krakow.

# Appendix

**I. Family Genealogy:**
Nika Fleissig, born Bronislawa Felicia Kohn, May 27, 1920

Family last seen in Wielicka, Poland, September 1, 1942

    Mother - Amalia (Mala) Bierman Kohn – April 15, 1897

    Father - Benjamin (Beno) Kohn 22 July, 1887

    Brother - Yosef (Toldek) Berthold Kohn, Feb. 27, 1923

# FROM MIRACLE TO MIRACLE

## II. Maps of Poland and Germany:

POLAND 1921-1939

— Poland's national boundaries
--- provincial boundaries
ŁÓDŹ provincial capital
Radom major town or city
**Wieliczka** Places Mentioned in Book
✠ Extermination Camp

# APPENDIX

Germany Partitioned in 1945 at the End of World War Two into
English, American, French, and Russian Sectors

# End Notes and
# Historical Information

[1]Poland had been part of the Austro-Hungarian Empire regaining its independence in 1918 at the end of World War I. Polish men who had served in the Austrian army and were veterans of World War I believed that their status as decorated soldiers would protect them from being killed. Unfortunately, the loyalty of Jewish citizens did not provide them any protection. Despite their service, they were simply classified as Jews and were subjected to deportation and murder.

[2]See maps in Appendix. Nika's parents and brother were probably transported to Belzec, a death camp situated in the southwest corner of the country on the Lublin-Lvov railway line. It was the most lethal of all Nazi camps established in occupied Poland. Unlike concentration camps where meticulous records were kept of arrivals, registration, prisoner numbers, work assignments, and deaths of each prisoner, no records were kept at Belzec. Perhaps this was because the people transported to Belzec were murdered immediately upon arrival. In this camp there was no trace of the victims.

From Hitler's initial rise to power in 1933, concentration camps were used as an instrument of Nazi persecution, first to house political prisoners, who were considered enemies of the regime. The Nazis instituted gassing installations to kill the handicapped, ill, or otherwise labeled unfit to foster the goal of achieving the "purity of the Aryan race." Increasingly, additional groups were slated for death by starvation and inhumane treatment: Jews, gypsies, homosexuals, and others who were deemed undesirable.

Slave labor camps were established, where the forced labor of inmates was used to advance the German war efforts. Prisoners who could no longer work and who were thus no longer useful, were shot, gassed, or disposed of by other means, including starvation and lack of medical treatment. As methods of killing became increasingly efficient, gassing rather than shooting was increasingly utilized for mass murder. In a sense, all of the hundreds of concentration camps were death camps in that thousands of inmates were executed for alleged crimes, were worked to death, or died from starvation or from exposure to the elements or diseases.

In 1942 a new type of camp was established made no pretense of utilizing the labor of prisoners, and instead was created as a death camp for the immediate extermination of masses of people by means of gas chambers and crematoria for disposing of the remains. Three such death camps were constructed for the murder of the Jews in German-occupied Poland: Treblinka, Sobibor, and Belzec. All of these were remote from major population centers and were situated next to major railways lines so that the killing operation could proceed quickly, efficiently, and with maximum secrecy.

From February through December 1942, close to half a million Jews were killed in its gas chambers by the German SS and their collaborators. The overwhelming number of those murdered in this death camp came from Lublin and the provinces of Krakow, Lvov, the heart of Galician Jewry. In the spring and summer of 1942 massive deportations began and by mid-1943 the Jews of Poland had been almost entirely obliterated. Once the Nazis concluded that all the Jewish communities of Galicia had been destroyed, they dismantled the death camp and tried to remove all traces of their crime.

Edited from correspondence with Professor Michael Berenbaum, Holocaust historian, during March of 2010, and Middle Tennessee State Univerity (Feb. 1996). *The Camps*. The Holocaust\Shoah Page. Retrieved March 8, 2010 from http://frank.mtsu.edu/~baustin/holocamp.html.

# FROM MIRACLE TO MIRACLE: A STORY OF SURVIVAL

[3]It is important to differentiate between the Warsaw Ghetto Uprising in 1943 and the Warsaw Uprising which took place one year later. The Ghetto Uprising, from April 19, 1943 until about mid-May, was a brave but desperate move in view of a planned annihilation of the quarter into which thousands of Jews had been herded. From the point of view of military strategy it was a hopeless struggle against well equipped German forces, and yet it displayed courage, strength, and a valiant will to show armed resistance and a heroic fight to the death on the part of Jews who defied the military might of the Nazi machine.

The Warsaw Uprising, described in several chapters of this book, was started on August 1, 1944 by Polish nationalists as the Soviet army was approaching Warsaw. The Russians were already at the Vistula River to the east, so an assault on Warsaw seemed imminent. The idea was to liberate the city before Soviet arrival and to underscore Polish sovereignty by meeting Soviets on equal terms. The underground Polish Home Army, which was loyal to the Polish government-in-exile stationed in London, had long planned some form of insurrection against the Nazi occupiers. The initial plan of the Home Army was to link up with the invading forces of the Western Allies as they liberated Europe from the Nazis. But at this point it became apparent that the Soviets, rather than the Western Allies, would reach the pre-war borders of Poland before the Allied invasion of Europe made much headway. The insurgents planned to reinstate Polish authority and leaders before the Soviet Polish Committee of National Liberation could assume control. The Poles and Soviets, although both fighting the Nazis, distrusted each other. The Poles wanted to be the ones to liberate Warsaw from German control themselves, and to set up a democratic government. They wanted to prevent the Russians from liberating the city and installing a pro-Russian, Communist regime in post-war Poland. However, the Polish army made several miscalculations, since the Polish leadership did not know that the American President, Franklin Roosevelt, had already agreed with Stalin to cede Poland and other parts of Europe to Russian control. Nor did they know that Roosevelt had promised to let Stalin annex parts of Poland to Russia proper. The Soviets, therefore, felt no urgency in moving on Warsaw quickly, and actually hindered drops of arms, food provisions, and supplies to the Polish Resistance forces on the ground. Nor did the Russian forces allow the Allies to use the surrounding air fields under Russian control, but rather gave the Germans the opportunity to destroy the Polish Home Army. Airdrops of food and supplies had to be made by planes using bases in the United Kingdom and Italy, greatly reducing their loads and effectiveness. Any supposed Allied support for the Warsaw Uprising was a sham.

> – Correspondence with Aaron Breitbart, Wiesenthal Center, Los Angeles, CA in February, 2010, and information from Wikipedia on the Warsaw Uprising

[4] The surrender was negotiated on October 5, 1944. The German General Rohr recognized the right of Home Army insurgents to be treated as combatants. The Wehrmacht promised to treat Home Army soldiers - men and women - in accordance with the Geneva Convention, and to treat the civilian population humanely. Together with earlier damage from the invasion of Poland in 1939, the Warsaw Ghetto Uprising in 1943, and the systematic bombing in response to the Warsaw Uprising, over 85% of the city was destroyed by January 1945, when the Soviets finally entered the city.

[5] The Hague Convention of 1907 and the Geneva Convention of 1929 stated that captors should treat prisoners in the same way their own soldiers were treated. The Geneva Convention documents contained assertions of the right of prisoners to receive food and medical aid, letters, and certain protections from physical harm and forced labor.

[6] The Soviets had not signed the Geneva Convention of 1929. That is probably why the Russian prisoners of war were treated differently by the Germans. They didn't received Red Cross packages, and were sent out to work for the German war effort.

[7] Eye witness account of Irena Skrzynska, one of the women prisoners of war in Oberlangen in online article: "A Brief Outline of the History of Women

# FROM MIRACLE TO MIRACLE: A STORY OF SURVIVAL

POWs from the Polish Home Army (AK) Held in Stalag VIC at Oberlangen after the Warsaw Uprising":

"The story of the soldiers of the Polish Home Army (AK) who fought in the Warsaw Uprising in August and September 1944 did not end with the capitulation of 2nd October of that year. Instead what ensued was a new episode in their lives in the POW camps dispersed throughout the territories of the Third Reich.

While the Warsaw Uprising lasted, the fate of insurgents captured by the enemy varied. In its very first weeks those captured were treated as plain 'bandits' and, if not immediately shot in Warsaw, they were either deported to concentration camps or to the German interior to do forced labour.

"However, the London based Polish Government-in-Exile's determined interventions did affect the terms and conditions of the act of capitulation, which acknowledged combatant rights to the men and women who had fought in the Uprising. This meant that the insurgents had prisoner-of-war status and were therefore interned in German *Stalags* or *Oflags*. Supervision of these prisoners lay exclusively in the competence of the German armed forces called the *Wehrmacht*. The capitulation document granted equal rights to both male and female prisoners. This was the first case in history where women found themselves behind the barbed wire of a POW camp.

"At the start of the Uprising, on 1st August 1944, there were approximately 5,000 women in the Warsaw AK. They had the same rights and duties as the men. They took part in all of the AK's activities: in the administrative and logistic services, as nurses or couriers, in sabotage as well as in the spreading of information and propaganda. If caught by the Germans, they could expect the same fate as their brothers in arms: the firing squad, prison or the concentration camp....

"In December 1944 the Germans started to send women prisoners from the Polish Home Army to Penal Camp (*Strafflager*) VI C in Oberlangen.

# FROM MIRACLE TO MIRACLE

"A hardship shared by all the women POWs were the deplorable living conditions at the various camps. The German authorities were simply not prepared to take in a couple of thousand women with special prisoner-of-war status. The male prisoners were sent to camps that had been functioning since 1939 and were automatically put under the care of the International Red Cross. The women, on the other hand, were kept in overcrowded barracks separated from the main POW camps by barbed wire. In these cramped conditions, cold, frequently hungry, and lacking even the most basic sanitary facilities, these women had to endure the severe winter of 1944-1945. Yet they resisted persistent threats and coercion to renounce their prisoner-of-war status and become civilians, for according to the Geneva Convention of 1929, as captured combatants, they could not be forced to work in support of the Third Reich's war effort....

"Among those interned there were women with higher education, polyglots, artists as well as other activists in culture and education. Thus series of lectures, discussions and various other cultural events were organised in order to liven up the intellect and avoid psychological breakdowns.

"In December 1944 the Germans started sending AK women prisoners to *Strafflager* (Penal Camp) VI C in Oberlangen. 5,000 women took part in the Warsaw Uprising, 3,000 of them were interned as POWs and 1,721 of these ended up in Oberlangen.

"The camp had already had a dark history. Situated in the marshy Emsland area of northwest Germany, it had been one of the many concentration camps set up in the years 1933-1938 to hold opponents of the Nazi regime. After the outbreak of World War II the camp was taken over by the *Wehrmacht* and began to hold POWs from the occupied countries of Europe. The harsh climate, slave labour, hunger and disease turned the camp into a place of death.

"In October 1944 Oberlangen *Strafflager* VI C was struck off the POW camp register on account of totally inadequate living conditions. Therefore the

# FROM MIRACLE TO MIRACLE: A STORY OF SURVIVAL

International Red Cross in Geneva was unaware of the fact that women POWs were later to be interned there.

"The Germans continued to regard the Oberlangen facility as a penal camp and started to send women members of the AK there as a punishment for being obdurate rebels who had refused work as civilians in the German war industry.

"The conditions in which we had to endure the winter of 1944-1945 were very difficult: two hundred prisoners in each rotten wooden barrack, draughty doors and windows (some lacking windowpanes), three-tier bunks, thin palliasses [mattresses] and only two cast-iron stoves burning damp peat that produced more smoke than heat. In one barrack there was a row of metal troughs with taps from which water, when there was any, barely trickled, and behind it two rudimentary latrines, all of which amounted to the camp's entire sanitary facilities. Eight barracks were designated for the healthy inmates, while at the front of the camp there was a hospital barrack, the camp kitchen, a sewing workshop, a bathhouse and a delousing station – of which I do not remember the last two ever functioning. One barrack was used as a chapel, while two more were left empty. These we exploited as an extra supply of fuel: we took out planks from the bunks, pulled up floorboards and even removed door and window frames until the camp authorities started imposing severe penalties for destroying government property.

"The food was the same as in other camps: in the mornings and evenings a tepid herbal tea, frequently mouldy bread, the occasional piece of margarine or a spoonful of beetroot marmalade. At midday we would receive soup from bitter cabbage or grubby peas with two or three jacket potatoes.

"The final stages of the war had a disastrous effect on supplies. Red Cross parcels from previous camps arrived in only very small quantities, if they were not stolen by the Germans or spitefully held at Lathen Railway Station some 12 km away....

# FROM MIRACLE TO MIRACLE

"The key to getting on with one another in Oberlangen was not only a matter of discipline but also of solidarity and camaraderie. In January 1945, when the first ten children were due to be born, for there were women who had become pregnant before leaving Warsaw, 'Commandant Jaga' announced at roll call: 'A baby is to be born, and it will be naked because its mother has nothing.' These words were enough: every woman who had anything to spare – a piece of bed linen, a handkerchief, a blouse or an undergarment – would undo the stitches, cut, sew and wash. So many bonnets, baby gowns and nappies were made for the first child that there was also enough for those who were born later. Cartons from Red Cross parcels were converted into cradles….

"With the coming of spring the Germans stepped up their efforts to win us over. One day a man arrived who the camp authorities introduced to us as Hitler's personal friend. For three days he tried to convince our Polish commander of Germany's good intentions towards Poland and to us in particular. He wanted us to form a women's legion that would fight against the Red Army. Our authorities advised this man to first gain permission from the Home Army Commander-in-Chief, General Bór-Komorowski, who was still being held in the Reich as a prisoner-of-war.

"Some time after the ineffective visit of the Füehrer's friend a group of German officers arrived to try to persuade our command to testify that we had been treated in accordance with the Geneva Convention. The group was headed by the commanding officer of all the POW camps in the region, who tried to persuade our commanders to withdraw a report, due to be sent to Geneva, on the offensive way in which Lt Treiber had treated our Commandant 'Jaga'. On that occasion he told her 'I spit on the Geneva Convention' and then fired in her direction – fortunately he missed. The increasing number of visitors was a sign that the end of the war and Germany's defeat were fast approaching.

"At 18.00 hrs on 12th April 1945 the Oberlangen camp was liberated by soldiers of General Maczek's 1st Armoured Division. The immense joy of being liberated by a Polish force was to last for weeks, but at the time the war was still on and we would have to wait another month before the women soldiers of the Polish Home Army and former POWs in the Third Reich could start the next chapter in their lives."

http://www.polishresistance-ak.org/16%20Article.htm

[8]See map in Appendix showing American, British, and Russian zones in post-war Germany. Note location of Oberlangen POW camp in Germany, near the Dutch border. Right after the war Nika traveled from Oberlangen to Antwerp, Belgium, to Frankfurt, Germany, and back to Belgium, before embarking on the S.S. Richardson transport ship to America.

[9]See Bibliography for more sources on Children of the Holocaust and Children of Survivors of the Holocaust.

# Bibliography of Suggested Books on Children of the Holocaust and Children of Holocaust Survivors

Auerbacher , Inge. *I Am a Star: Child of the Holocaust.* New York: A Puffin Book, Penguin Group, 1993.

Buergenthal, Thomas and Elie Wiesel. *A Lucky Child: A Memoir of Surviving Auschwitz as a Young Boy.* New York: Little, Brown, and Co., New York, 2007.

Epstein, Helen. *Where She Came From: A Daughter's Search for Her Mother's History.* New York: Penguin Putnam, 1997.

Epstein, Helen. *Children of the Holocaust: Conversations with Sons and Daughters of Survivors.* Putnam, 1979, Paperback: Penguin, New York, 1988.

Fremont, Helen. *After Long Silence.* New York: Dell Publishing, 1999.

Gruener, Ruth. *Destined To Live: A True Story of a Child In The Holocaust.* New York: Scholastic, Inc., 2007.

Harris, Mark Jonathan and Deborah Oppenheimer. *Into the Arms of Strangers: Stories of the Kindertransport.* New York/London: Bloomsbury Publishing, 2000.

Hass, Aaron. *In the Shadow of the Holocaust: The Second Generation.* London: Tauris Ltd., 1991.

Hoffman, Eva. *After Such Knowledge: Where Memory of the Holocaust Ends and History Begins.* Cambridge, Massachusetts: Perseus Books Group, 2004.

Karpf, Anne. *The War After: Living With the Holocaust.* Oxfordshire, England: William Heinemann Ltd., 1996.

Liebrecht, Savyon. *Apples from the Desert.* London: Loki Books, Ltd., 1998.

Perl, Toby Appleton. *Secret Lives - Hidden Children and Their Rescuers During WWII.* New York: Fox Lorber Studies. (DVD - July 20, 2004)

Schroeder, Peter W. *Six Million Paper Clips: The Making of A Children's Holocaust Memorial.* Minneapolis, Minnesota: KAR-BEN Publishing, 2004.

# BIBLIOGRAPHY

Spiegelman, Art. *Maus I: A Survivor's Tale: My Father Bleeds History*. New York: Pantheon Books, 1973.

Volavkova, Hana. *I Never Saw Another Butterfly*. New York: Schocken Books, 1993.

Zullo, Allan, and Mara Bovsum. *Survivors: True Stories of Children in the Holocaust*. New York: Scholastic Inc., 2004.

Photo of Michael (Mechl) and Gusta Bierman's 12 descendents with their spouses taken at the wedding of the youngest daughter Sala, in the mid-1920's

Nika's parents are in 2nd row far right. Her Aunt Ruth and Uncle Arnold Licht are in top row, far right.

Top Row: HUDZIA & Salomon, SALOMEA SYMCIA (MUNDA) Birman & Moses Leser Johannes, LEJZER (Bachelor), KALMAN (Bachelor), RUTH ( RUZIA) &Arnold Licht

2nd Row: HINDA & Bernard, AREK & Klara, PAULA & Shaiku, AMALIA (MALA) & Benjamin (BENO) Kohn

Bottom Row: HANIA & Shimon, GUSTA BIERMAN, Young couple: SALA & Mulek, MECHL BIERMAN, SARA & Janek

Mother
Amalia Bierman Kohn

Father
Benjamin Kohn
(This photograph was kept in
Nika's  shoe throughout the war.)

Brother "Toldek" & Father
Benjamin "Beno" Kohn

Brother "Toldek" and Nika 1942

Cousin Anita Johannes, Brother "Toldek", & Nika

Nika "Bronia" Kohn 1934, age 14

Nika in Krakow 1938

Nika (center) with school friends in Krakow 1938, age 18

# HANDWERK u. KUNST

### ARBEITSGENOSSENSCHAFT n. A. ● WARSCHAU C 1, KREDYTOWA 9

BÜRO: KREDYTOWASTR. 9
FABRIK: TREBACKASTR. 10

Jetzt: Ord.ntr. (Bracka) Nr. 18
Fernruf: 242-01
242-05

FERNRUF: Büro: 657-48
Fabrik: 207-03
BANKKONTO: WARSCHAUER
DISKONTOBANK, KONTO 3663

### BESCHEINIGUNG.

| IHRE NACHRICHT VOM | UNSER ZEICHEN | TAG |
|---|---|---|

Warschau, den 1 Juni 43.

Wir bescheinigen hiermit, dass Frl. Maria

### ŻYLIŃSKA

geb. am 20.4.1920, wohnhaft, Warschau, Sniadeckich
12.4.23, bei uns als Telefonistin beschäftigt ist.

Unsere Firma ist ausschliesslich auf Ausführung von
kriegswichtigen Aufträgen für Heeresdienststellen
eingestellt und wir bitten, der Obengenannten bei
der Ausübung ihrer Tätigkeit keine Schwierigkeiten
zu bereiten.

Arbeitsgenossenschaft
„HANDWERK u. KUNST."
m. Anteil.
WARSCHAU

Es wird hiermit bestätigt, dass die obige Firma
für die Heeresstandortverwaltung Warschau, kriegs-
wichtige Aufträge ausführt.
Es wird gebeten, die Obengenannte zu anderen Ar-
beiten nicht heranzuziehen.

CERTIFICATE
=======================

Warsaw, June 1, 1943.

We hereby confirm that miss Maria

ZELINSKA

born April 20, 1920, living in Warsaw, Suideckich 12 w 23, is employed by us as switchboard operator.

Our company is exclusively here to carry out orders important to the war effort and the army, and we ask that no difficulties be made for the above person in the performance of her duties.

Workcooperative

HANDWERK U. KUNST
Signature

It is hereby confirmed that the above company carries out orders for army headquarters in Warsaw which are important to the war effort. We ask that the above person will not be enlisted in any other project.

STAFF PAYMASTER AND MANAGER
Signature

English translation of German document authorizing "Maria Zylinska" to work in Warsaw, 1943.

Nika in Wieliczka, 1942

Nika as nurse
"Maria Zylinska,"
Warsaw, 1944

Still as Maria Zylinska 1945
after Liberation in Polish Red
Cross Uniform

Nika inFrankfurt, 1945 as
"Belgian" Civilian Hired by
G-2 American Intelligence
while awaiting passage to
America

Nika shortly after liberation from Prisoner of War camp in 1945, wearing Polish uniform

Polish passport issued by Polish consulate in Belgium under real name, Bronislawa Felicia Kohn, on the last day before Communists took over Poland and the Consulate office was closed down.

KONSULAT
RZECZYPOSPOLITEJ POLSKIEJ
w BRUKSELI
CONSULAT
DE LA RÉPUBLIQUE DE POLOGNE
à BRUXELLES

N°: 5869/45.

BRUKSELA, dnia
BRUXELLES, le
13, rue de Florence
Tel. : 37.40.92 – 37.41.68

C E R T I F I C A T.

--------------------------

        .Le Consulat de Pologne à Bruxelles certi-
fie par la présente que ce jour, s'est présentée à ce
Consulat, Melle Bronisława-Felicia KOHN, de nationalité
polonaise, née le 27 Mai 1920, à Rzeszów, fille de Benjamin KOHN et de Amalia BIERMANN, épouse KOHN, qui a
déclaré que, pendant l'occupation allemande, elle a porté
le faux nom de ŻYLINSKA Maria, pour se soustraire aux
persécutions allemandes.

        Elle a présenté le témoin Georges DINEUR,
domicilié à Berchem-Anvers, 16 rue des Cinq Bains, qui
connait sa famille et a affirmé ses dires.

        Le présent certificat est délivré à la
demande de l'intéressée, pour être présenté au Consulat
des Etats-Unis, en vue de faire les démarches pour obte-
nir le visa d'entrée.

Bruxelles, le 26 Septembre 1945.

                    Pour LE CONSUL DE POLOGNE,

                    Z. KULESZA
                    Vice-Consul.

French document, issued at the Polish Consulate in Belgium
officially restoring Nika's identity, September 26, 1945.

R E S T R I C T E D

HEADQUARTERS
U.S. FORCES, EUROPEAN THEATER

WH./mct
(MAIN) APO 757
26 December 1945

AG 300.4 (20 Dec 45) L-217.

SUBJECT: Orders.

TO : BRONISLAWA KOHN, Allied Civilian.

1. Miss BRONISLAWA KOHN, Belgian civilian, attached this Hq.,(Counter-Intelligence Corps), will proceed from her present station on or about 26 December 1945 to Brussels, Belgium.

2. Travel by military vehicle and/or rail transportation is directed.

3. The cost of transportation will be borne by the War Department.

4. The travel directed herein has been cleared in compliance with Cir 146, Hq US Forces, European Theater, 29 Oct 45.

5. TCNT. TDN. 60-115,105 P 431-02 A 212/60425.

BY COMMAND OF GENERAL MCNARNEY:

WILLIAM H. WRIGHT,
OFFICIAL
Asst Adjutant General

DISTRIBUTION:
4 - Miss Kohn
1 - Hq.970th CIC Det.
2 - Civilian Pers.

R E S T R I C T E D

Document from Allied Headquarters in Frankfurt stating that Bronislawa Kohn has permission to travel by U.S. official military transportation. December, 1945.

GHENT
159, BLD. DU GAZOMÈTRE
TELEPH. 597.54 - 595.29
TEL. ADDR.: LYKESBEL

# Lykes Bros. (belgium) SOC. AN.

FORMERLY SOC AN BELGE DELTA

*Lykes*  *Lines*

Rég Comm. Antwerp : 1413

ANTWERP
39. LONGUE RUE NEUVE
TELEPH : 292,14 - 230,47
TEL. ADDR.: LYKESBEL
COMPTE CHÈQUES : 5325

DP/JV.

Antwerp, December 31st. 1945.

To the American Consulate General,
Antwerp.

DUPLICATE

Dear Sirs,

Subject: Passage to the United States.

We hereby confirm having booked for a passage
to the United States on board of a W.S.A. vessel, name
still unknown, provided all consular formalities have
been fulfilled

Miss Bronislawa KOHN.

We expect to be able to embark this Lady
in the period of the validity of her visa.

This office will take care of informing your
Services of the name of the vessel on which passenger
embarks and the sailing date.

Yours very truly,
Lykes BROS.(belgium) SOC.ANON.
Passenger Agents for the U.S.
War Shipping Administration.

A.F.DE RUYTER,
Traffic Department.

Authorization of passage to the United States on board a ship for
sometime after December 1945, once the American troops had
had been transported home to the States.

# Polish Girl, Heroine of Underground, Wants to be a Dress Designer

Still wearing a WAC uniform, an attractive brown-haired Polish girl, who worked with the underground and later for American Army Intelligence, arrived in Philadelphia today with hopes of a new career.

"I want to be a dress designer," said Miss Nika Kohn, 23, a native of Warsaw, as she stepped off the cargo vessel Edward Richardson, which arrived today at Pier 100 South, below Oregon Ave., from Antwerp. The ship also carried ten war brides.

Her desire to become a dress designer was aided by her aunt and uncle, Mr. and Mrs. Arnold Licht, of Forest Hills, Long Island, who were on hand to greet her at the dock. Licht is in the textile business in New York.

**Family was Killed**

Miss Kohn, who speaks fluent English, said that she was in Warsaw in 1939 when the Germans captured the city. Her mother, father, and brother, were killed.

She joined the underground movement which resisted the Nazis, and in August 1944, became a nurse and Polish forces inside the city. In October she was captured by the Germans when the Poles staged an uprising and tried to break out of Warsaw to meet the advancing Russians.

Sent to a German prison camp at Oberlung[sic] Miss Kohn was freed by the British last March. She was transferred to Belgium where she volunteered to serve with the American Army.

**Put in WAC Uniform**

They put her in a WAC uniform and stationed her at Frankfurt where she was assigned to the intelligence section.

Nika Kohn,
Heroine of the Polish underground,
the 23-year-old former nurse hopes
to become a dress designer.

Note: Nika's aunt told her to say she was younger than her real age, which was 26. The reporter got the place and dates a bit mixed up. Nika was still in Krakow in 1939.

Alfred Fleissig

Alfred & Nika Fleissig, Wedding Day 1946

Bella White (Cousin)
& Ruth Licht (Aunt)

Nika, April 5, 1946
Atlantic City Honeymoon

Alfred Fleissig with Ruth
and Arnold Licht, 1960's

Alfred & Nika Fleissig with Daughter Alicia

William Berthold Fleissig & Alicia Susan Fleissig 1952

Top: Sofia Pozniak being honored at Yad VaShem, Jerusalem, Israel Dec. 5, 1979.

Bottom: Ala Wachtel, Nika's childhood friend, on right, helping to plant tree for Mrs. Pozniak on "Avenue of the Righteous Gentiles"

Alfred, Nika, Alicia and Itzhak, at Magal wedding Israel 1974

Nika, Itzhak, Alicia,
Amir and Tali Magal, 1983

Tali, Itzhak, Nika, Alicia, Amir
at Amir's Bar mitzvah 1991

Nika with Andrew Casper 1990's

Nika with Andrew at North
Pole for Nika's 80th
Birthday May 27th, 2000

Nika's son, Will Fleissig, and his bride Wendy Kohn
at their wedding in Aspen, Colorado, September 22, 2001

Nika with her grandchildren

From left: Ariel Kohn, David Ferrell, Nika,
Amir and Tali Magal, Mia Kohn.

Family Gathering at Nika's Art Exhibit, Wellfleet, Massachusetts, 2008
(L to R) Itzhak Magal, Amir Magal, Craig Fleishman,
Alicia Magal, Wendy Kohn, Will Fleissig, David Ferrell, Irene
Goldberg, Tali Magal holding Mia Rose Kohn,
And Nika seated holding Ariel Kohn.

Generations of women: Nika, granddaughter Tali Magal, daughter-in-law Wendy Kohn, daughter Alicia Magal

Nika with Daughter Alicia on Mother's Day

Nika in her studio 2008

Tali Magal and Craig Fleishman with Nika at their wedding,
August 1, 2010, Cape Cod, Massachusetts.

Late 19th century Silver Kiddush cup from Nika's home in Poland. It was buried in the earth during the war, retrieved by a cousin and returned to Nika in America, used for Shabbat and holidays when Alicia and Will were children, then cherished by Alicia all the years her children were growing up. Now this heirloom cup is handed down to Tali Magal to treasure in her family in years to come.

Alicia giving Tali the "maternal kiddush cup"
on Shabbat before her wedding

CPSIA information can be obtained
at www.ICGtesting.com
Printed in the USA
BVHW071926271221
624891BV00001B/96